TAX ANSWERS AT A GLANCE

Instant answers, advice and tips from the experts

**H M Williams Chartered
Certified Accountants
and Associates**

Tax Answers at a Glance

by H M Williams Chartered Certified Accountants and Associates

First published in 2001 and published thereafter annually by Lawpack Publishing Ltd

20th edition published jointly by St Edward's Press Ltd and Lawpack Publishing Ltd

© 2021 Ashley Smith, Iain Watson, Tim Smith, Hugh Williams, and Lawpack Publishing Ltd

ISBN 978-1-913714-09-3
Ebook ISBN 978-1-913714-10-9

Printed in Great Britain

Contents

About the authors

Tax Answers at a Glance was first published in 2001. It has since become the annual work of a team of tax experts who work, or who have worked, at H M Williams in Plymouth. For over 30 years, the firm and its partners have been writing books that demystify business topics, particularly on tax, company law and business development. During this time the firm has won three national awards: *The Daily Telegraph* award for the professional firm with the best customer service, the 2020 award for being the most innovative medium-sized accountancy firm, and the Butterworth Tolley award for being the small to medium-sized firm with the best tax team in the country.

Important information

Welcome to *Tax Answers at a Glance*. It is packed with information and advice on your obligations and rights as a taxpayer.

The information this book contains has been carefully compiled from professional sources, but its accuracy is not guaranteed as laws and regulations may change in the Budget and be subject to changing interpretations. Please be aware that many of the details referred to in this book have been announced by the Chancellor of the Exchequer in various Budgets and other official announcements. Such measures are not always passed into law.

Tax regulations are stated following the Budget announcements made on 3 March 2021 in London and related statements made in Edinburgh.

Throughout *Tax Answers at a Glance*, reference to spouses includes same-sex registered civil partners.

Neither this, nor any other publication can take the place of tax or other advice provided by a professional accountant. Common sense should determine whether you need the assistance of an accountant rather than relying solely on the information provided in this book.

Coronavirus

2020 saw the arrival of the Coronavirus pandemic and the announcement by the Chancellor of the Exchequer of a series of unprecedented measures and assistance to help those in business, and others. When trying to write the edition that should have been published in 2020, the authors did their best to keep up with the details of these measures, but the constant flow of the measures meant that we were constantly having to amend the text; so constantly, that we decided that it would not be possible to produce a book that we could stand by. We feared that no sooner had the book been printed than it would need yet another amendment.

This year, 2021, we have decided to produce the book in the same way as it has always been produced, which means focussing on the tax, etc., changes that the Chancellor of the Exchequer announced in his Budget. We believe this to be only sensible. What this means is that, with the ever-changing nature of what has to be described as an economic crisis, readers should be extra-diligent before taking action as a result of reading this book.

Introduction

There are many books on tax, for both the professional and lay reader, but our impression is that most of them seem to look rather heavy, even if they are not. As practising accountants, we know only too well how clients will phone us with questions (perhaps quite simple questions) and all they want is a simple answer, and quickly.

With this having happened over nearly 50 years in practice, we have come to the conclusion that there must be a lot of taxpayers who don't engage the services of a professional accountant, and who have similar questions they would like answered.

This book intends to answer all such questions.

It has been written deliberately to home in on the questions we are most asked, giving the answers at a glance, rather than all the background details which, to be realistic, most taxpayers don't want or need.

With this book being updated annually, we invite readers to submit any questions that this book does not address, and we will try to include their suggestions in the following edition. If you should have any such suggestions then please send them by email to: info@stedwardspress.co.uk or by post to St Edwards Press Ltd, 20 Barra Close, Highworth, Swindon, Wilts, SN67HX.

Stop press!
Major changes for all taxpayers ahead

We begin this edition of *Tax Answers at a Glance* by telling you that, as a taxpayer, you need to be aware that the most far-reaching changes are being made to the way that information is submitted to Her Majesty's Revenue and Customs (HMRC); and these changes really do concern everybody.

Possibly the most significant change will be, as we are told by HMRC, the disappearance of the annual income tax return. We have yet to be told of the details of what it will be replaced by, but even if the full details have yet to be announced, it would quite wrong to begin this tax guide without warning you about this fundamental development. In the view of the authors, these changes are the most major changes that any of us accountants have seen in our entire working careers.

But, as you are about to read, it doesn't end with the disappearance of the income tax return.

All the changes that we are referring to here come under the heading of:

Making Tax Digital (MTD)

so you need to remember that name and its initial letters because we are all going to hear a lot about MTD in the years ahead.

The key events and dates of implementation are as follows:

April 2019	Most VAT-registered traders with turnover exceeding the threshold must keep digital records and submit their VAT returns by MTD.
April 2021	Digital links must be in place. This means that if you are using MTD for your VAT submissions, you must not copy figures and paste them into the software that you use to make your VAT submissions.
April 2022	All VAT-registered traders must use MTD to submit their VAT returns.
April 2023	All self-employed business and landlords with turnover above £10,000 must report under MTD, and do so quarterly.

April 2024   Companies can start using MTD for Corporation Tax

April 2026   All companies will join MTD for Corporation Tax

Please refer to our new chapter, number 19, where we explain MTD in more detail.

CHAPTER 1

Tax in general

'Our new Constitution is now established and has an appearance that promises permanency; but in this world nothing can be said to be certain, except death and taxes.' So wrote Benjamin Franklin in 1789 and it is true that taxes have been with us for a very long time.

Today, we have a huge range of different taxes which we list below. There are direct taxes on income and on capital including property and there are indirect taxes on expenditure such as Value Added Tax and excise duties. We did have one Chancellor of the Exchequer, Nigel Lawson, who promised to abolish one tax in every Budget, but the rest have been constantly on the lookout for new ways of getting our money, ideally without us noticing, so-called stealth taxes. Recent examples include Insurance Premium Tax and Airport Passenger Duty.

What constitutes a 'good' tax system?

There are five basic conditions against which a tax system should be judged:

- **Fairness.** This means that everybody should pay a fair share. First, people in the same financial circumstances should pay the same amount. Second, people should pay according to their means: taxes should be progressive and not regressive. Income Tax is progressive because richer people pay higher rates than poorer people. In fact, the most recent data shows that 43% of adults pay nothing, while the top 1% pay more than a quarter of the entire Income Tax bill. The Community Charge – better known as the Poll Tax – which the Government sought to introduce back in 1990 was regressive because each adult, with few exceptions, was expected to pay the same amount

- **Adequacy.** This means that taxes should raise enough money to pay for public services. In practice, most governments struggle to balance the books and fill the gap by borrowing.

- **Simplicity.** This means what it says on the tin: taxes should be uncomplicated, easy to understand, calculate and pay.

- **Transparency.** This means there should be as much information as possible about the tax system in the public domain: we should know how many people are paying, how much they are paying, what the reliefs are costing and so on.

- **Ease of collection.** This be means that it should not be too cumbersome or expensive to collect taxes and that they should be difficult to evade.

Tax avoidance and tax evasion

Some taxes are imposed in order to change our behaviour; for example, the sugar tax that is levied on soft drinks, but most are designed solely to raise revenue. Of course, they too may well change out behaviour as we seek to find ways around them. The best historical case of tax avoidance was that of the window tax: when householders were taxed on the number of windows in their house, they simply blocked some of them up and you can still see evidence of that in some Georgian buildings.

There is an important distinction between tax avoidance and tax evasion. The latter simply means the intentional defrauding of the tax authorities, while tax avoidance is all about finding a legitimate way to minimise your tax liabilities. In a landmark court case in 1936, a judge said that: 'Every man is entitled, if he can, to order his affairs so that the tax attaching under the appropriate Acts is less than it otherwise would be. If he succeeds in ordering them so as to secure this result, then, however unappreciative the Commissioners of Inland Revenue or his fellow taxpayers may be of his ingenuity, he cannot be compelled to pay an increased tax.' This straightforward ruling has since been weakened by subsequent judgments which have looked at the overall effect of a series of transactions and ruled that, if a transaction had pre-arranged artificial steps that served no commercial purpose other than to save tax, the proper approach was to tax the effect of the transaction as a whole. But there will probably always be an ongoing battle between taxpayers and the tax authorities in this area.

In this book, we look at the different taxes we have to pay and at the legitimate allowances and reliefs that are available to us but we do not condone artificial tax avoidance schemes.

The different taxes that we have to pay

Between us (private individuals and businesses, etc.), we pay the following taxes:

Direct taxes

- Income Tax
- National Insurance Contributions
- Capital Gains Tax
- Inheritance Tax
- Stamp Duty
- Stamp Duty Land Tax
- Corporation Tax
- Petroleum Revenue Tax

Indirect taxes

- Value Added Tax
- Fuel Duty
- Tobacco Products Duty
- Spirits Duty
- Wine and Made-Wine Duty
- Beer Duty
- Cider Duty
- Soft Drinks Industry Levy
- Machine Games Duty
- Gaming Duty
- General Betting Duty
- Pool Betting Duty
- Bingo Duty
- Remote Gaming Duty
- Lottery Duty
- Air Passenger Duty
- Insurance Premium Tax
- Landfill Tax
- Aggregates Levy
- Climate Change Levy

- Bank Levy
- Bank Surcharge
- Horserace Betting Levy
- Customs Duty
- Excise Duty
- Vehicle Excise Duty
- Business Rates
- Council Tax
- Annual Tax on Enveloped Dwellings

It's quite a list, isn't it? A summary of the current tax rates and allowances is provided in Appendices 1 and 2.

This table shows the income from the above taxes that the government expected and expects to raise in the following tax years:

	2019/20 £bn	2020/21 £bn	2021/22 £bn
Income Tax	193	208	198
Corporation Tax	60	58	40
Petroleum Revenue Tax	(1)	-1	0
Capital Gains Tax	9	11	9
Inheritance Tax	6	6	6
Stamp Duty	4	4	3
Stamp Duty Land Tax	13	14	12
Value Added Tax	156	161	151
Fuel Duties	28	28	26
Tobacco Duties	9	9	10
Spirit Duties	4	4	4
Wine Duties	4	4	4
Beer and Cider Duties	4	4	4
Air Passenger Duty	4	4	1
Insurance Premium Tax	6	7	7
National Insurance	142	150	147
Climate Change Levy	2	2	2
Other HMRC Receipts	7	9	9

Vehicle Excise Duties	6	7	7
Bank Levy and Surcharge	2	4	2
Business Rates	31	32	24
Council Tax 36	38	40	
Other Taxes and receipts	34	91	84
Interest and Surpluses	51	19	30
Overall Total Income	**810**	**873**	**820**

This table shows the ways in which the government planned and plans to spend the taxes that it raises:

	2019/20 £bn	2020/21 £bn	2021/22 £bn
Health	166	178	230
Social Protection and Personal Social Services	290	321	342
Public Order and Safety	35	38	41
Defence	52	55	60
Education	103	116	124
Interest	43	56	45
Housing	32	32	33
Transport	37	44	51
Industry, Agriculture and employment	25	30	70
Others including EU transactions	58	58	57
Total government spending	**841**	**928**	**1053**

Based on these figures, there will be a deficit in 2021/22 of about £233 billion. This overspend is known as the public sector borrowing requirement, or PSBR.

Changing the tax rates

Recent governments have changed the method of deciding when tax rates should be changed (in other words, they have hopped about a bit and no more so than in 2019, 2020 and 2021), but normally the announcements of the tax rates are given in the Autumn Budget Statement in November.

Those rates and allowances usually come into force on 6 April immediately following.

When it comes to National Insurance, these changes are also announced in the autumn Budget. This gives HM Revenue & Customs (HMRC) and employers the chance to be prepared for the changes some months later.

The Chancellor has sometimes announced changes to other taxes for future years (i.e. beyond the immediately succeeding year) in his Budget and so, to a certain extent, taxpayers and tax advisers have known a few tax rates for a considerable period in advance. One example is the announcement in the March 2021 Budget that Corporation Tax will rise to 25% in 2023.

The Income Tax year

The Income Tax year runs from 6 April in one year to 5 April in the next. One of the authors of this book spent a considerable amount of time badgering HMRC, Chancellors and Treasury officials to change this cumbersome system by using a more sensible date. Since Corporation Tax and VAT end their financial years on 31 March, it would make sense for the government to move the Income Tax year by a few days so that all three-year ends are coterminous.

The reason the tax year ends on 5 April is not a logical one, and this is our understanding of how it came about: In the old days, and we are talking hundreds of years ago, the tax year began on 25 March (the Feast of the Annunciation or Lady Day). Up to 1752 there were two European calendars and they had drifted apart by a few days. Britain used the Julian Calendar, devised at the time of Julius Caesar, while the rest of the Continent (pretty well all the rest) used the Gregorian Calendar (introduced by Pope Gregory the Great), which meant that by the time we had reached 1752, the Continent was 11 days ahead of us. In that year, the two calendars merged and Britain 'lost' 11 days. The Treasury said that it could not afford to lose 11 days' worth of income and so added 11 days on to the end of the tax year. This meant that the tax year in 1753 ended on 4 April.

In 1800, our Treasury, for some reason, thought that there was a leap year. The formula for leap years is that they are years which can be divided by four and, when there is a centenary year, when they can be divided by 400. the year 1800 could not be divided by 400 to give a whole number result and so it was not a leap year – our Treasury thought otherwise. So the Treasury added an extra day to the tax year at that stage resulting in a tax year end of 5 April.

Tax and civil partners

All the tax legislation that applies to married couples also applies to civil partners. For instance, civil partners are able to transfer assets to each other without incurring any Capital Gains Tax.

If they have two main residences, they can only have one Principal Private Residence exemption, so they may wish to consider making an election to nominate the main residence. They are also able to transfer assets to each other free of Inheritance Tax.

Throughout this book any reference to married couples includes civil partners.

Business rates and Council Tax

A tax on the occupation of non-domestic property, **Business rates** are collected by local councils. They keep 50 per cent and pay the other 50 per cent over to central government. The central share is then distributed back to the councils via revenue support grants. Business rates are assessed on the area of space occupied by businesses.

Council Tax is collected by local councils and goes towards the following local services:

- Planning and economic development
- Recreation and tourism
- Environmental health
- Refuse collection
- Education
- Social Services
- Police
- Fire

Council Tax in England and Scotland is assessed on the market value of domestic properties, as at 1 April 1991. In Wales, the valuation date is 1 April 2003. Properties are then graded in bands A to H. There is a 25 per cent discount where only one person lives in a property. There can be a 100 per cent Council Tax surcharge if a property has been empty for more than two years or 200 per cent if a property has been empty for five years. Councils can give Council Tax discounts for second homes and, in Wales, they can also charge premiums.

There is no Council Tax in Northern Ireland. Instead, rates are levied on the capital value of properties as at 1 January 2005.

HM Revenue & Customs and HM Treasury

HM Revenue & Customs (HMRC) is the government department that is responsible for collecting most of the nation's taxes. HMRC advises the Treasury on tax matters generally, but it's the Treasury, controlled by the government in power at the time, that decides how much tax it wants to raise from taxpayers. It then works with HMRC to devise a system that enables that money to be collected.

Within HMRC, there are Inspectors of Taxes, who check that the correct amount of tax is being paid by individuals, trusts and companies. There are also debt recovery people, who make sure that the tax is paid.

CHAPTER 2

Income Tax

Income is the sum of all the wages, salaries, profits, interest payments, rents, and other forms of earnings received in a given period of time. A tax was first charged on income by William Pitt the Younger in 1799. It was supposed to be a temporary tax to cover the cost of the Napoleonic War but it is still with us.

Income Tax is charged on:

- Trade profits (including all business profits)
- Property income
- Savings and investment income
- Employment income
- Pension income
- Mineral royalties
- Miscellaneous income (covers income not falling under the other headings)
- Pension income (which includes taxable Social Security benefits)

Income Tax is not charged on:

- Adoption Allowance
- Annuities from gallantry awards
- Attendance Allowance
- Bereavement Support Payment
- Best Start Grant
- Betting, lottery and pools winnings, and raffle prizes
- Child Benefit (While Child Benefit is not taxable, if your household receives it and someone in your household has taxable income of over £50,000, they may have to pay extra tax.)
- Childcare vouchers

- Child dependency additions
- Child Tax Credit
- Child Trust Funds
- Children's savings accounts ('Junior ISAs')
- Christmas bonuses paid by the state to pensioners
- Cold Weather Payments
- Compensation for loss of employment of up to £30,000 (professional advice must be sought)
- Compensation for mis-sold personal pensions
- Compensation paid to Equitable Life policyholders
- Council Tax Benefit
- Damages and compensation for personal injury, including interest
- Disability Living Allowance
- Educational Maintenance Allowance
- Electricity microgeneration for home use (Feed In Tariffs)
- Employment & Support Allowances (income related)
- Foster Care Income (within certain limits)
- Funeral Support Payment
- Gifts for employees from third parties if they are under £250 a year
- Gratuities and bounties from the armed forces
- Guardian's Allowance
- Health costs including eye tests, prescriptions, travel under the Hospital Travel Costs Scheme
- Home improvement, repair and insulation grants
- Housing Benefit
- Incapacity Benefit (short-term – lower rate) for first 28 weeks
- Income Support, unless you are on strike when you claim
- Individual Savings Accounts (ISAs)
- Industrial injury benefits
- Insurance bond withdrawals of up to five per cent per year (this can be complicated and professional advice should be sought)
- Insurance policy payments (mortgage payment protection, permanent health, etc.)
- Interest from National Savings Certificates
- Interest on overpaid tax
- Invalidity pensions

- Life assurance policy bonuses and profits
- Long-service awards of up to £50 for each year of service (for employees)
- Lump sums from an approved pension scheme (up to 25%)
- Lump sum bereavement payments
- Maintenance or alimony payments
- Maternity Allowance
- Miners' Coal Allowance
- National Savings Certificates' increase in value
- Pension Credits
- Personal Independence Payments
- Pensions from Austria or Germany to victims of Nazi persecution
- Premium Bond prizes
- Provident benefits paid by a trade union of up to £4,000 for lump-sum payments
- Purchased life annuities – capital element only
- Rent-a-room relief up to £7,500 a year
- Return to Work Credit
- Save As You Earn Schemes (SAYE) bonuses and interest
- Scholarship income and bursaries
- Severe Disablement Allowances (if originally claimed before 2001)
- Share option profits made under an SAYE option scheme – Capital Gains Tax may be payable
- Shares awarded under an approved Share Incentive Plan (professional advice must be sought)
- Social fund payments including budgeting loans, funeral expenses payments and Sure Start Maternity Grants
- Statutory Redundancy Pay
- Strike and unemployment pay from a trade union
- Student loans & educational grants
- Suggestion scheme awards up to £150.
- Tax Reserve Certificates
- Training allowances for reserve forces
- Travel to work on a works bus
- TV licence payment for over 75s
- Universal Credit

- Vaccine damage payment
- Venture Capital Trust dividends
- War Disablement Benefits
- War Widows' & Widowers' Pension
- Winter Fuel Payments
- Woodlands income
- Working Tax Credit
- Young Carer Grant

The rates of Income Tax

In 2021/22, Income Tax is payable at the following rates:

'The savings rate' and 'The dividend rate' – 0 per cent on the first £1,000 of interest income (reduced to £500 if you are a higher rate taxpayer), and £2,000 of dividend income.

'The basic rate' – 20 per cent of your taxable income, up to £37,700.

'The dividend rate' – 7.5 per cent on dividend income falling within the basic rate band, but in excess of the £2,000 dividend tax allowance.

'The higher rate' – 40 per cent on the next £37,701 – £150,000 of taxable income, other than dividends.

'The higher dividend rate' – 32.5 per cent on dividend income falling in the higher rate band, but in excess of the £2,000 dividend tax allowance.

'The additional rate' – 45 per cent on taxable income, other than dividends, in excess of £150,000.

'The additional dividend rate' – 38.1 per cent on taxable income consisting of dividends in excess of £150,000 after the £2,000 dividend tax allowance.

Also, the Starting Rate for Savings of 0% on the first £5,000 of interest may be available for those whose other sources of income are £17,500 or less. Every £1 of income above your personal allowance reduces your starting rate for savings by £1.

Personal allowances

The rates of personal allowances for 2021/22 are:

Personal	£12,570*
Blind Person's	£2,520

*the personal allowance in 2021/22 is gradually withdrawn for income over £100,000 at a rate of £1 of allowance lost for every £2 over £100,000.

Scottish Income Tax

Income Tax rates and allowances in Scotland now differ quite significantly from those in England, Wales and Northern Ireland. The Scotland Act 2016 confers on the Scottish Parliament the power to set all Income Tax rates and the thresholds of bands (above the Personal Allowance) that apply to the non-savings and non-dividend income of Scottish taxpayers.

On 25 February 2021, the Scottish Parliament set the following Income Tax rates and bands for the 2021/22 tax year. These assume that the taxpayer is in receipt of the standard UK Personal Allowance:

Scottish bands	Band name	Scottish rate (%)
£12,570 - £14,667	Starter	19
£14,667 - £25,296	Basic	20
£25,296 - £43,662	Intermediate	21
£43,662 - £150,000	Higher	41
More than £150,000	Top	46

The rest of the UK	Band name	Rate (%)
£12,570 - £37,700	Basic	20
£37,701 - £150,000	Higher	40
More than £150,000	Additional	45

Welsh Income Tax

From April 2019, the Welsh Government has had the authority to make changes to the rates of Income Tax payable by Welsh taxpayers. For the year ended 5 April 2022 the rates of tax charged in Wales are the same as those charged in England. The amount of the Personal Allowance and the different tax rate bands are all the same as in England.

The Personal Tax Return

This can be completed manually or it can be submitted online.

Some taxpayers (mostly employees and pensioners) are now being issued with a shorter, simpler Short Tax Return (SA200). The taxpayer won't need to calculate his own liability, even if the Tax Return is submitted to HMRC after 30 September.

Paper Tax Returns must be filed by 31 October; Returns filed online must reach HMRC by 31 January and by 31 December if they want their unpaid tax to be collected through their notice of coding. Late filing may result in one or more penalties.

Generally speaking, you will have to complete a Tax Return if you:

- are self-employed earning more than £1,000;
- are in partnership;
- are in receipt of net income from land and property of more than £2,500 (or less if the tax cannot be dealt with through the PAYE coding system);
- incur taxable capital gains;
- earn over £50,000 pa and have children for whom Child Benefit is received.

And very importantly, if you:

- are sent one (if HMRC issues a Tax Return or a Notice to complete a Tax Return, it has to be completed by the taxpayer).

If in any doubt, contact HMRC, advise them of your circumstances, and get them to confirm whether you should fill out a Tax Return.

If you need to get hold of a Tax Return, download one from the HMRC website. A checklist of what to keep for your Tax Return is provided at Appendix 3.

Simple Assessment

From the 2016/17 tax year HMRC have introduced a simpler system for paying tax, aimed at taxpayers who are within self-assessment, but with 'simple' affairs. One does wonder why, if their affairs are that simple, they are within self-assessment! In any event, a taxpayer in self-assessment has to complete a Tax Return, and only when this is submitted to HMRC can HMRC really know all about the taxpayer's affairs in that year.

Since 2016/17 HMRC have a new scheme for certain taxpayers whose affairs are simple, whereby, since HMRC believe that they hold all data needed to calculate a taxpayer's liability, taxpayers will simply be sent a tax calculation (P800) and a demand for payment.

Taxpayers who fall into this category should beware that HMRC regularly issue tax calculations that do not take into consideration the entirety of a taxpayer's affairs. If you receive a tax calculation from HMRC, check it carefully – or ask an accountant to do so.

Calculating the tax due

If you have to complete a Tax Return, included in the package will be a tax calculation guide for you to follow. The main thing to bear in mind is that if you get your Tax Return submitted by 31 October each year, HMRC will work out for you how much tax you have to pay and when you have to pay it.

In principle, you make two payments a year.

1. On 31 January each year you will pay the balance of the previous year's tax still owing plus, if your liability for the year is in excess of £1,000, one half of the previous year's tax liability as a first payment on account for the following year.

2. On 31 July each year you will pay the second half of last year's tax liability as a second payment on account. On 31 January following, you will find yourself paying any balance of tax that is due plus another payment on account based on this year's total tax bill, and so on.

Tax paid late

An interest charge is (i) automatic on late paid Income Tax, Class 4 National Insurance contributions and Capital Gains Tax, and (ii) added to existing liabilities and treated as tax due and payable.

A surcharge applies to all amounts due in respect of the previous tax year on 31 January following the end of that tax year and not paid within 30 days. This is five per cent of the amount unpaid more than 30 days after the due date with a further five per cent of the amount unpaid more than five months after the 30 days. Another five per cent surcharge arises if the tax remains unpaid after eleven months after the 30 days. However, the taxpayer may appeal against a surcharge if he has a reasonable excuse for non-payment.

HMRC has the power to take money directly from the bank account of anyone who owes tax of more than £1,000, and has the means to pay it, but refuses to do so. This will only be taken if you repeatedly refuse to pay what you owe, you have received a face-to-face visit from HMRC to discuss your debt and you would have at least £5,000 in your account after they have taken the debt. The taxpayer has 30 days in which to appeal against this action if he believes the figure is incorrect.

Tax Returns not filed on time

If you have been issued with either a Self-Assessment Tax Return to complete, or a Notice to file a Tax Return, there are two important deadlines. If you are submitting a paper Tax Return, this has to be filed with HMRC by 31 October following the end of the tax year. If you are filing an electronic return, the deadline is 31 January following the end of the tax year. If you fail to submit your Return by the appropriate deadline, even if by only one day, you will receive a £100 penalty. This is regardless of whether or not you owe any tax.

Once the Return is three months late, daily penalties of £10 are charged up to a maximum of £900. Once the Return is six months late, a charge of either five per cent of the tax due or £300, whichever is the greater, is charged. Once the Return is 12 months late, a further penalty of five per cent or £300 (whichever is the greater) is charged. In serious cases the penalty can be increased to 100 per cent of the tax due.

Please note, however, that if you are issued with a Self-Assessment Tax Return at any other time of the year apart from the bulk issue in April, that Return will have its own submission deadline, which may extend beyond 31 October and 31 January. The Return will show the filing deadline which applies to it and the penalties mentioned above will still be enforced if this specific deadline is not adhered to.

Allowances and deductions that can be set against taxable income

Most taxpayers are entitled to a personal allowance. Apart from that it all depends on a taxpayer's personal circumstances. Here are just some examples of the reliefs available:

- Relief for losses in a business
- Relief for certain professional subscriptions and expenses
- Relief for personal pension contributions
- Relief for Gift Aid payments
- Relief for investments made under either the Venture Capital Trust, Enterprise Investment or

Enterprise Investment Schemes
- Blind Person's Allowance
- Relief for interest on money borrowed for certain purposes
- Business expenses
- Relief for losses on the sale of certain shares

From April 2017, a trading allowance and a property allowance have been introduced in the sum of £1,000 each; see details later in this book.

There is a cap on some of the reliefs you can claim. This is set at the higher of £50,000 or 25 per cent of an individual's income. The reliefs subject to the cap are:

- trade loss relief against general income and early trade losses relief;
- property loss relief (relating to capital allowances or agricultural expenses);
- post-cessation trade relief, post-cessation property relief, employment loss relief, former employees' deduction for liabilities, losses on deeply discounted securities and strips of government securities;
- share loss relief, unless claimed on Enterprise Investment Scheme (EIS) or Seed Enterprise Investment Scheme (SEIS) shares; and
- qualifying loan interest.

Earned and unearned income

Currently unearned income suffers less tax than earned income because earned income (salaries, wages, benefits, etc.) is not only taxable but is also subject to National Insurance contributions.

The distinction between the two is not a key one nowadays, but one of the more obvious distinctions arises in the case of a director shareholder. If a director is paid a salary, then, like nearly all people in employment, both the company and the director must pay National Insurance Contributions on that salary. The payment of (say) an additional £1,000 as earnings may result in about 45 per cent of that figure (basic rate tax, employers' NI and employees' NI) going to the government. If that same person is paid a dividend of £1,000 out of taxed profits, no further tax will be due to the government although, in due course, there will be tax payable by the director when it comes to completing his personal Tax Return, if his total dividend income for the year exceeds £2,000.

Married Couple's Allowance

(Please beware, this is complicated.)

Married couples of whom one was born before

6 April 1935   **£9,125

** tax relief is restricted to 10%.

The income limit for Married Couple's Allowance is £30,400 and the full allowance of £9,125 is reduced by £1 for every £2 that total income exceeds this figure. The Married Couple's Allowance cannot be reduced below £3,530. To claim the Allowance, complete the relevant section on the Tax Return.

Marriage Allowance

Since 6 April 2015, it has been possible, in certain circumstances, for married couples and civil partners to transfer some of their personal allowance to the other spouse/civil partner:

In the 2021/22 tax year, the amount that can be transferred is £1,260.

The transferable amounts are fixed, you cannot transfer more or less than these amounts. In 2021/22, the transfer is worth £252 to the recipient.

You can only receive the Marriage Allowance if you are liable to tax at the basic rate. If you are liable at the higher or additional rates, the transfer is not permitted. If you or your partner were born before 6 April 1935 and are eligible for the Married Couple's Allowance, this may be more beneficial than the Marriage Allowance.

In order to obtain the Marriage Allowance the transferor needs to either:

- complete the relevant sections of their Tax Return to inform HMRC they wish to transfer part of their personal allowance; or
- apply online to inform HMRC they wish to transfer some of their personal allowance; or
- phone HMRC and inform them.

Unfortunately, there is no provision for the claim to be made on the recipient's tax return.

Tax relief on payments of interest

Opportunities to claim tax relief on payments of interest on loans are limited and are now restricted to the following:

- buying a share in a partnership or contributing capital to a partnership if you are a partner;
- buying shares in an unlisted trading company or lending capital to it;
- buying plant and machinery for use in a job or partnership.

The interest paid (and not the capital) is deducted from your total income in the year of payment.

Tax relief on mortgage interest

If the purpose of your mortgage was to buy your own home, you cannot get tax relief on the mortgage interest.   But, if you mortgage your house in order to buy a rental property, you can set off the mortgage interest against your rental income. However, from 6 April 2017, there are limitations placed upon the amount of relief that can be claimed; see 'What are the new rules for buy-to-let landlords?' in chapter 7.

Income Tax when someone dies

You must report a death to HM Revenue and Customs (HMRC) as soon as possible if you're dealing with the tax affairs of someone who's died. HMRC will tell you if you need to fill in a Self Assessment Tax Return on the deceased's behalf. When someone dies, they are entitled to their normal full year's worth of allowances for the period from 6 April up to the date of death.

Income arising after death is treated as the income of the estate of the deceased person and becomes the responsibility of the trustees or executors. What they need to send depends on the size of the estate, and the money that came from it during the administration period.

They must fill in a trust and estate Tax Return if any of the following apply:

- the total Income Tax and Capital Gains Tax due for the administration period was more than £10,000;
- the estate was worth more than £2.5 million at the date of death;
- more than £500,000 a year came from the sale of the estate's assets.

If the trustees or executors do not need to send a Tax Return, they can make 'informal arrangements' instead. To do this, they need to write to HMRC and tell them:

- the Income Tax and Capital Gains Tax due for the administration period;
- the name, address, National Insurance number, and Unique Tax Reference of the deceased
- their name and contact details.

When the estate is distributed, both the capital and the income that has arisen since the date of death will be distributed according to the Will to the various beneficiaries and tax will be deducted from any income that has been received at the appropriate rate.

Beneficiaries in receipt of income that has been credited to a deceased person's estate, will receive that income net of basic rate tax, and while this income may be liable to higher-rate tax, there is also a chance that you might be able to claim some back or there may be no adjustment one way or the other. Beneficiaries should be issued with Form R185 ('Estate income'), which shows both the net payment and the tax paid.

Income of children and Income Tax

Children, from the moment they are born, are entitled to a personal allowance and if they are in receipt of net income they are almost certainly entitled to a repayment of tax. Accordingly, where children are in receipt of income that has not arisen on money received from a parent, and from which tax has been deducted, it's potentially refundable. Get a tax claim form from the Tax Office or download it from the HMRC website (note that it's called a Claim for Repayment of Tax Deducted from Savings and Investments (R40) and not a Tax Return, but it amounts to the same thing). When you have completed it and sent it in, HMRC will either send a cheque in favour of the child or make a refund of tax straight to that child's own bank or building society account. The parent can also receive the refund on the child's behalf.

Tax efficient investments for children

A savings account should be opened with building societies or banks that are in the children's name. There are also Junior Individual Savings Accounts (JISAs) which are specifically aimed at children.

It's quite permissible for children to hold shares in companies.

If the children don't have any investments and if the parents have surplus after-tax income of their own which they give to their children, this is usually tax free in the children's hands and, if the parents are particularly wealthy, is a very useful way of transferring income to them, so that the children can accumulate a sum that can then be invested. However, once the income from the source exceeds £100 p.a. it will be taxed in the hands of the parents. Where parents transfer their own shares to their children, if the children are under 18, the income arising on these shares will be regarded as belonging to the parents, so this doesn't save tax.

The Child Trust Fund was a tax-free savings scheme designed for children born between 1 September 2002 and 2 January 2011. The government contributed £250 when the child was born and a further £250 (£500 for lower-income families) at the age of seven. Parents, family and friends could contribute a further £1,200 annually. The child was entitled to the fund at the age of 18 and there were no restrictions on how he used the money.

Children born after 2 January 2011, who are therefore not eligible for a Child Trust Fund, can invest in a Junior ISA (JISA). There is no tax to pay on any interest or gains made by a JISA. The JISA can invest in cash or stocks and shares. The total amount which can be invested is £9,000 in the year ending 5 April 2022. When the child becomes 18, he can withdraw the investment for any purpose.

Charitable giving and Income Tax

- Gifts of money to charities attract tax relief under the Gift Aid scheme. The gift is treated as if it had been made after deduction of Income Tax at the basic rate. So if you give £80 to a charity, it can get £20 tax back. As a basic rate taxpayer, the making of the gift serves to extend the basic rate band by the gross equivalent of the payment. If you are a higher-rate taxpayer, you can claim a further £20 (or £25 if your top rate of tax is 45 per cent) of tax relief in your Tax Return.

- You need to complete a Gift Aid declaration. If you turn to Appendix 5, you will see an example of this and how it works. However, remember this will only work if you have paid more tax than will be reclaimed by the charity. Otherwise, HMRC will send you a bill for the difference.

- There is a generous tax relief for gifts of certain investments and property to charity.

Do be aware, however, that if a non-taxpayer makes a Gift Aid contribution, then they will be creating a tax liability for themselves in the amount of the tax relief which the charity is reclaiming.

Payroll Giving

If their employer is registered under the Payroll Giving scheme, employees can arrange a regular deduction from their pre-tax pay to go to a nominated charity, church or charitable association.

Employers need to sign an administration contract with an authorised Payroll Giving Agency. They do make a small administration charge that is either deducted from the donation or can be paid separately by the employer (around four to five per cent).

Reclaiming overpaid tax

If you are likely always to pay too much tax (through receiving no gross income, i.e. all your income suffers tax at source), HMRC will spot this and send you a tax claim form, R40 ('Claim for repayment of tax deducted from savings and investments'). This will be returnable to a Tax Office that deals solely with tax repayments. This scenario is frequently encountered by the young and the elderly.

If, on the other hand, you normally pay tax but in a certain year discover that you have overpaid, tick the appropriate box on the Tax Return and you can claim for the money to be refunded to you. If you leave the overpayment un-refunded, it will go to reduce your future year's tax payments. Generally speaking, the repayment will be processed more quickly if paid directly into a bank/building society account rather than if paid by cheque.

Pre-owned assets

Although this is not a common occurrence and is dealt with in more detail under the Inheritance Tax chapter, please be aware that this is a charge to Income Tax not Inheritance Tax.

This is a tax charge that is applied to the benefit people get from the free or low-cost enjoyment of assets they formerly owned or provided the funds to purchase but have now 'given' away.

The charge applies to both tangible (land, property, possessions, etc.) and intangible assets.

This will primarily affect people who have entered into 'contrived arrangements' to dispose of valuable assets while retaining the ability to use them. This is most frequently encountered in Inheritance Tax avoidance schemes where property is given away but please be aware, this is a charge to Income Tax not Inheritance Tax.

There are specific exceptions to the charge:

- The property ceased to be owned before 18 March 1986.
- The property formerly owned is currently owned by your spouse or civil partner.
- The property was sold at open market value and paid for in cash.
- The asset still forms part of the individual's estate for Inheritance Tax purposes under the gift with reservation rules.
- The asset was only owned by virtue of an inheritance which has subsequently been varied by agreement with the beneficiaries (i.e. a deed of variation).
- Any enjoyment of the asset is incidental, or arises after an out-and-out gift to a family member and comes to the benefit of the donor because of unforeseen changes in the donor's circumstances.

The amount of the tax charge will be based on the rental value for land and property, and five per cent of capital value for possessions and intangible assets, subject to a de minimis limit of £5,000.

As it may be impossible to withdraw from potentially complex transactions from the past, an election can be made to have the value of the asset included in the estate for Inheritance Tax purposes. This will avoid an Income Tax charge becoming due. You should take professional advice if you think this applies to you.

Personal Tax Account

HM Revenue & Customs (HMRC) introduced the Personal Tax Account (PTA) in 2015 to make it easier for people to view and manage their personal tax affairs online.

It provides a range of services, allowing you to check your state pension, submit claims for tax rebates, file Tax Returns and manage tax credits.

But research shows many taxpayers are not taking the opportunity to check on their tax affairs. 46% have never checked their personal tax accounts, despite nearly a third (29%) wanting a better understanding of their tax affairs.

Your PTA is a way to view and manage your tax affairs in one secure place.

There are a range of services available with more being added all the time.

You can use your personal tax account to:

- check your Income Tax estimate and tax code
- fill in, send and view a personal Tax Return
- claim a tax refund
- check and manage your tax credits
- check your State Pension
- track tax forms that you've submitted online
- check or update your Marriage Allowance
- tell HMRC about a change of address
- check or update benefits you get from work, for example company car details and medical insurance

You can create a PTA at www.gov.uk/personal-tax-account.

CHAPTER 3

National Insurance

A limited system of National Insurance was introduced by Prime Minister Lloyd George in the National Insurance Act 1911. For the first time, workers were insured against sickness and unemployment. Then, after the Second World War, Prime Minister Attlee introduced what we now know as the welfare state, a much more comprehensive programme of pensions, sickness, unemployment and other benefits. Successive governments have built on this so that today, as the table on page 5 shows, social security and social services cost some £342 billion per year.

National Insurance Contributions

National Insurance contributions are an extra and important tax that has to be paid on certain sources of income. As the table on page 4 shows, they account for £147 billion of Government revenues, the third largest source but nowhere near enough to cover the costs of £342 billion. That is because, while some benefits are contributory, many are not. The original idea was that you would pay into a ring-fenced National Insurance Fund and your benefits would, in due course, come out of that fund. While there is still a National Insurance Fund, it is not particularly meaningful because the contributory principle has constantly been chipped away at. Indeed, it is often now completely overlooked. For example, there has been recent political pressure to make the self-employed pay the same contributions as the employed notwithstanding the fact that the self-employed cannot claim Jobseeker's Allowance.

The contributions paid are, in principle, used to pay for an individual's following state benefits:

- State Retirement Pension
- Bereavement Allowance
- Bereavement Payment

- Widowed Parent's Allowance
- Maternity Allowance
- Jobseeker's Allowance
- Employment and Support Allowance

The different classes of National Insurance?

There are four classes of National Insurance and some have subdivisions.

- **Class 1** primary contributions are paid by employees on their earnings. Secondary contributions are paid by their employers on the same amount. Class 1A contributions are paid by employers on their employees' benefits in kind. (See also 'Providing benefits for my employees', page 45.) Class 1B contributions are paid by employers where they decide to pay the tax on their employees' benefits under a so-called PAYE Settlement Agreement.

- **Class 2** contributions are paid by the self-employed whose earnings from self-employment exceed the annual threshold. The self-employed also may be liable for Class 4 contributions.

- **Class 3** contributions are voluntary. You can pay them in order to protect your benefits, if you are not otherwise paying National Insurance contributions (e.g. this might arise because you have no earnings on which National Insurance is payable, but you still want to pay for a state pension).

- **Class 4** contributions are additional contributions paid by the self-employed, whose earnings exceed a certain sum. Class 4 contributions don't provide any further benefits for the contributor and are, in effect an extra National Insurance 'tax' and paid with Income Tax on the same dates as Income Tax.

The Rates of National Insurance – the basic facts for 2021/22

There are four classes of National Insurance contributions:

- **Class 1a.** For employees who pay 12 per cent of their earnings between £184 per week and £967 per week, and 2 per cent on all earnings over that figure.

- **Class 1b.** For employers pay 13.8 per cent on their employees' earnings over £184 per week. There is no upper limit.

- **Class 2.** For the self-employed with profits above £6,515 who pay £3.05 per week. This sum is now collected with the tax liability on 31 January.

- **Class 3.** This class is for those who do not fall into the above categories but who wish to pay voluntary National Insurance contributions of £15.40 per week. This class is for:

  - Those earning less than £120 per week
  - The self-employed with profits below £6,515
  - Those living abroad but not working and who have paid at least three years of NI contribution in the past

- **Class 4.** Again for the self-employed. Self-employed people with profits over £9,568 pay 9 per cent National Insurance on all profits between £9,568 and £50,270, and 2 per cent on all profits over that figure.

People over normal retirement age and children under 16 pay nothing. However, employers still have to pay 13.8 per cent on their earnings.

The methods of paying National Insurance contributions

- **Class 1** contributions are paid on a weekly or monthly basis by the employer (secondary contributions). The employer deducts its employees' contributions (primary contributions) from their gross pay (along with Income Tax and other deductions) and pays that sum to HMRC, together with its own contributions, by the 22nd of the following month when paying electronically (19th of the month for all other payment methods).

- **Class 2** are included with the self-assessment payments in January and July each year.

- **Class 3** As we have seen these are voluntary contributions. They are usually paid in a lump sum to HMRC.

- **Class 4** contributions are calculated along with the self-employed's self-assessment Income Tax calculation and paid once or twice a year, with the Income Tax payments.

Employment Allowance

Employment Allowance is an annual amount that is available to some employers to offset against their Class 1 National Insurance bill. It allows them to reduce their annual National Insurance liability by up to £4,000. They pay less employers' Class 1 National Insurance each time they run their payroll until the £4,000 has gone or the tax year ends (whichever is sooner). You can claim Employment Allowance if you're a business or charity and your employers' Class 1 National Insurance liabilities were less than £100,000 in the previous tax year.

The benefits of paying or being credited with National Insurance contributions

The table below gives you an indication of what the different classes of National Insurance contributions pay for:

Type of Benefit	Class 1 Employed	Class 2 Self-employed	Class 3 Voluntary
State Retirement Pension basic	Yes	Yes	Yes
State Retirement Pension additional	Yes	No	No
New State Pension	Yes	Yes	Yes
Bereavement benefits	Yes	Yes	Yes
Maternity Allowance	Yes	Yes	No
Contribution-based Employment & Support Allowance	Yes	Yes	No
Contribution-based Jobseeker's Allowance	Yes	No	No
Incapacity Benefit	Yes	Yes	No

National Insurance numbers

If you have lost your National Insurance number, you can find it through your Personal Tax Account and download a confirmation letter. If you still can't find it, you can fill in form CA 5403 ('Your National Insurance Number') and send it to HMRC in Newcastle or call the National Insurance numbers helpline on 0300 200 3500 and answer some questions.

Failing to pay National Insurance contributions

Make no mistake, this can be expensive either if you start up as an employer who fails to deduct tax and National Insurance contributions from your employees' wages, or if you start in self-employment and fail to register with HM Revenue & Customs (HMRC).

If, as an employer, you fail to pay over the correct National Insurance contributions for your employees by 22 April following the end of the tax year, not only will these have to be paid over, but in addition there will be interest due on the late payment and, in addition to that, there will be penalties for failing to make the payments on time.

If you are an employee whose employer is failing to deduct contributions from your pay and pay them over to HMRC, you cannot be held liable to make the payment yourself. It's the employer's responsibility. Our understanding of the law is that, since it's the employer's responsibility, there is no way in which HMRC can get you to pay the National Insurance contributions that should have been deducted from your gross pay nor should your benefits be affected, because HMRC will collect the contributions from your employer.

HMRC is responsible for National Insurance contributions. The application forms for the newly self-employed are designed in such a way that the National Insurance obligations are dealt with at the same time as registering for tax under self-assessment.

Once Class 4 contributions have been calculated on your Tax Return they become part of your overall tax liability and are thereafter no longer separately identified. Unpaid contributions are treated in the same way as unpaid tax.

Finding out if National Insurance contributions are not up to date

You should contact the Pensions Service and find out exactly where you stand with regard to contributions you have made and benefits you are entitled to. This is called a retirement pension forecast. There are three ways of getting this. You can either apply online at www.gov.uk/check-state-pension or you can call the Future Pension Centre on 0800 731 0175 and ask for a statement or you can fill in the BR19 application form, Application for a State Pension Statement, and send it by post.

You can generally make contributions for the previous 6 years if there are any gaps in your contribution record. The forecast will show you what can be done in this regard and what the impact will be on your pension entitlement.

Please note that you won't have to pay National Insurance contributions if you have reached state pension age. However, if you are still working beyond state pension age, your employer remains liable for their Class 1 contributions. The normal retirement age for both men and women is 66. It is going up from 66 to 67 between 2026 and 2028 for men and women born after 5 April 1960.

Over-paying and deferring National Insurance

There is a cap (the annual maximum) on the amount of contributions that an individual can pay in the tax year. The annual maximum may be reached if a person has more than one job or is simultaneously employed and self-employed. By contrast, there is no ceiling on employer contributions.

You can apply to HMRC for a refund of those contributions paid in excess of the annual maxima. There is no time limit for making such an application. However, HMRC will only refund contributions in excess of a minimum amount.

You may be concerned that you are going to pay too much National Insurance. This can happen if you have a number of employments or if you have both employments and self-employments. However, just having a number of sources of earned income does not mean that you must have paid too much, just that you might have paid too much. It all hinges on the amounts of your earnings and/or profits. To avoid this situation arising, you can apply for deferment of your Class 1 contributions. Deferment application forms can be downloaded from the HMRC website (www.gov.uk/defer-national-insurance) and the form needed is a CA72A. For the contribution year 2021/22, this must be submitted to HMRC by 14 February 2022 in order to claim a Class 1 deferment. If you expect to pay Class 1 contributions as an employee and Class 2 and/or Class 4 contributions as a self-employed person, then you do not need to apply or re-apply for Class 2 and/or Class 4 deferment. When you complete your Self Assessment Tax Return, HMRC will use the information they already hold along with the information you provide in your Tax Return to let you know about any Class 2 and Class 4 National Insurance you need to pay. Details of the amount to be paid will be shown on your self-assessment calculation.

National Insurance contributions on benefits in kind

Employers are required to pay Class 1A contributions at 13.8 per cent of all benefits, such as company cars and private medical insurance provided to their employees. If they pay their employees' tax on such benefits in accordance with a PAYE Settlement Agreement, they will also have to pay Class 1B contributions on that tax.

CHAPTER 4

Employment and Income Tax

Taking on an employee

Taking somebody on can be one of the early big milestones in any business. What follows can also apply to private individuals who are employing people such as cooks, nannies, gardeners, etc. and so, while most of what follows relates to the things that a businessperson should do, private individuals should be aware that they may well be caught by the PAYE regulations that relate to employing people.

There is no easy answer to this very simple question. Having said this, the only answer is that you have to obey the law but knowing what the law is, is not always easy in itself.

If you take on somebody and you are paying him more than £170 a week, no matter what his age, you have to pay employer's National Insurance contributions and the rate is 13.8 per cent. If this is the case, then the first thing you should do is inform HMRC that you have taken somebody on. You can do this by calling the New Employer Helpline on 0300 200 3200.

The second thing you should do is decide how you are going to handle the PAYE payment obligations. There are three possibilities:

1. Ask a professional accountant or payroll bureau to look after the PAYE side of things for you. Both will tell you how much to pay your employees net of tax and National Insurance each week or month and will also advise you how much your monthly or quarterly payments to HMRC are. Each will also be able to help you with the benefit forms (P11Ds).

2. Buy a simple computer program and do the work in-house yourself. These are good, economically priced and well worth the investment in both software and stationery.

3. **If you have fewer than 10 employees,** use the HMRC website, which has a tax and NIC calculator. The software provided free by HMRC is certainly worth considering but you cannot print out payslips from it.

If you take on someone earning more than £120 per week and less than £170 per week, National Insurance contributions won't be due but you still need to notify HMRC of his pay each week or month, so as to ensure that he qualifies for National Insurance credits. Paying someone over £120 per week also means that you are caught by the Real Time Information regime. This requires the employer to submit electronically pay details to HMRC on or before the date when payments are made to employees. This requirement can be dealt with by most PAYE software, or, if you have fewer than 10 employees, you can use the free software provided on the HMRC website.

If you take on someone earning less than £170 per week, while there may be no National Insurance Contributions to worry about, you may still find that you need to deduct tax from his earnings. This depends on the tax code you have been directed to use, which is either shown on Form P45 ('Details of employee leaving work') from his previous job or on Form P9 ('Notice to Employer of Employee's Tax Code').

We said at the start that there is no easy answer to this. Perhaps the best answer to give you is to discuss the matter with HMRC or with a professional accountant. Make no mistake, it is a complicated business and one that is very important to get right. Employers should not turn a blind eye to their obligations. HMRC also run courses to help employers comply with their obligations. With only a few exceptions, all employers are required to use online filing for PAYE.

Working out whether someone is an employee or self-employed

As with the previous question there is no easy answer to this. There have been many painful cases brought to light by a visiting HMRC PAYE investigator. Business owners who thought that all their people were self-employed have discovered to their horror and great expense that they should have been deducting tax and National Insurance from the gross payments that they have been making to their staff.

Below you will find a list of questions that you should ask which will help you decide whether the person whose services you are using is self-employed or an employee.

As practising accountants, we are of the opinion that, if somebody is 'engaged' on a regular basis, but is regarded by both parties as self-employed (and the following questionnaire justifies this decision), a contract for services should be signed by both parties which can be shown to HMRC and which clearly establishes that the arrangement is one of self-employment.

Employed or self-employed? A questionnaire to help you decide

HMRC is keen to classify self-employed people as employees because this increases National Insurance Contributions and Income Tax.

How can you tell if someone is an employee or is self-employed? Answering the following questions should help. Note that there are separate and new rules for workers in the construction industry; the following questions are not appropriate for such workers. (On the HMRC website there is an Employment Status Indicator that can be used as a guide, although it may still be worthwhile getting professional advice on the matter.) We must emphasise that these questions give an indication of status. The different points considered carry different weights in the overall decision, so if the overall result is marginal, it would probably be best to seek professional advice on the matter. There are many tax cases where people thought they were self-employed but a court or tribunal found that they were not, with expensive consequences.

1. Is there a contract of service, i.e. a contract of employment?

    A 'no' answer indicates self-employment.

2. Is there a contract for services, i.e. a notice supplied by the person carrying out the work (A), indicating the nature of goods or services he will provide to B (this need not be written)?

    A 'yes' answer indicates self-employment.

3. Is the person who does the work in business on his own account?

    A 'yes' answer indicates self-employment.

4. If the person is in business on his own account, has evidence been provided that this is indeed the case (e.g. copy accounts, the payment of Class 2 National Insurance contributions)?

    A 'yes' answer indicates self-employment.

5. Are the hours worked decided by the person doing the work?

    A 'yes' answer indicates self-employment.

6. Are the days worked decided by the person doing the work?

A 'yes' answer indicates self-employment.

7. Does the person doing the work decide when to take his own holidays?

A 'yes' answer indicates self-employment.

8. Does the business proprietor supervise the work?

A 'no' answer indicates self-employment.

9. Is the person part and parcel of the business?

A 'no' answer indicates self-employment.

10. Does the person supply tools and/or materials when he carries out the work?

A 'yes' answer indicates self-employment.

11. Does the person doing the work give the business an invoice for the work done?

A 'yes' answer indicates self-employment.

12. Does the business calculate how much to pay the person doing the work and give a payslip?

A 'no' answer indicates self-employment.

13. Is self-employment the intention of both parties?

A 'yes' answer indicates self-employment.

14. Is the person bound by the customer care credo of the business?

A 'no' answer indicates self-employment.

15. Is the person carrying out the work required to wear a uniform or dress tidily at the diktat of the business?

A 'no' answer indicates self-employment.

16. Is the person carrying out the work provided with a car or transport by the business?

A 'no' answer indicates self-employment.

17. In the event of sickness, does the business continue to pay the person while not at work?

A 'no' answer indicates self-employment.

18. Is the person carrying out the work at liberty to work for other businesses?

A 'yes' answer indicates self-employment.

19. Is the person carrying out the work required to work in order to perform a specific task?

A 'yes' answer indicates self-employment.

20. Does the business, on asking this person to carry out work for it, assume any responsibility or liability characteristic of an employment, such as employment protection, employees' liability, pension entitlements, etc.?

A 'no' answer indicates self-employment.

21. Is the person who does the work paid an agreed price per job?

A 'yes' answer indicates self-employment (i.e. he is not paid for the hours he works, but for the work carried out).

22. Is the work carried out regularly?

A 'no' answer indicates self-employment.

23. Does the individual work for other people?

A 'yes' answer indicates self-employment.

24. Does the person carrying out the work advertise?

A 'yes' answer indicates self-employment.

25. Does the person carrying out the work have headed stationery?

A 'yes' answer indicates self-employment.

26. Can the person send a substitute? If so, has this ever happened?

A 'yes' answer indicates self-employment.

27. Does the person have to rectify faulty workmanship in his own time and at his own expense?

A 'yes' answer indicates self-employment.

Having addressed these questions, you should now begin to know whether in reality the person under consideration is an employee or is self-employed. However, a definite answer can only be given by the courts and just because a worker is self-employed elsewhere, he can still be classed as an employee of yours.

PAYE

PAYE stands for Pay As You Earn. It represents a logical system whereby week by week or month by month an employer deducts tax in such a way that, at the end of the Income Tax year, the right amount of tax has been deducted and handed over to the authorities. It works in the following way:

Let us say that you earn £16,570 a year and your personal allowance is £12,570. Your rate of tax will be 20 per cent.

If you paid your tax just once a year, you would calculate the tax as follows:

- £16,570 less your tax-free personal allowance of £12,570 gives you:
- taxable pay of £4,000 on which:
- tax at 20 per cent is £800.

The way PAYE works is to collect that £800 on a weekly or monthly basis as follows:

Somebody with a tax allowance of £12,570 would be given a PAYE code of 1257. During the year, at whatever payment date you were making a wages or salary payment, an appropriate proportion of that £12,570 would be deducted by your software from the gross pay (in this example, either £241.73 for a weekly paid employee or £1047.50 for a monthly paid employee). This would then give the amount to be taxed at 20 per cent. So, for a weekly paid employee, you take the gross payment £318.65 less £241.73 equals £76.92, to be taxed at 20%. So the PAYE is £15.38; and £15.38 x 52 weeks = £799.96 which is near enough to £800. For a monthly paid employee, it would be gross £1,380.83 less the tax free element of £1,047.50, equals £333.33 to be taxed at 20%. So the monthly PAYE is £66.66; and £66.66 x 12 = £799.92, which is also near enough to £800.

Tax codes and notices of coding

A tax code is a code number representing the tax-free part of an employee's income, assigned by HMRC for use by employers in calculating the tax to be deducted under the PAYE system. A notice of coding is issued by HMRC and states your current tax code as calculated by HMRC. A PAYE notice of coding is also known as a form P2 and is usually posted at the start of each tax year by HMRC. It explains how HMRC calculates the employee's tax code. A much simpler document, simply giving the tax code (P9), will be handed to the employer so that he knows which tax code to apply to the employee's pay.

In other words, a simple answer is – a tax code is a number given to an individual which enables the employer to work out how much tax to deduct and a notice of coding is the piece of paper on which that number has been printed by the tax authorities.

The dangers of failing to operate PAYE

This can be very nasty. Employers who fail to operate PAYE properly can find that, when they are found out (and they will be found out!), they have to pay over not only the tax and National Insurance contributions that should have been deducted, as well as the National Insurance contributions that they, as employers, should have been paying, but also interest on the late payment if it was paid after 19 April following the end of the tax year and a penalty of up to 100 per cent of the tax for not having done it properly in the first place.

Don't fail to operate PAYE properly. However, if you discover an innocent error, contact HMRC at once and they will give you guidance on sorting it out.

The records that an employer must keep

A proper system for keeping employees' records consists of the following:

For each employee:

- A contract of employment
- Job description
- Notices of PAYE coding
- A permanent data sheet recording the employee's full name, home address, date of birth, National Insurance number, gender, hours worked, date of joining, dates of pay rises, etc.

Employers certainly have a number of important obligations. Our view is that, if employers are doing their job properly, they will want to keep their records properly, pay their people properly and keep within the law. In our experience it's businesses that behave in such a manner that succeed and flourish.

Real Time Information (RTI)

RTI is designed to give HMRC accurate and up-to-date information about what employees are earning. It also allows HMRC to ensure that it is receiving from employers the correct amount of tax, National Insurance and any other deductions that are due. It represents a transformation in the way that employers operate their PAYE arrangements and has facilitated the implementation of Universal Credit.

Fundamentally, every time an employee is paid the employer must make an electronic submission to HMRC giving details of the employee, the amount paid to them, the deductions made from the payment and also details of the hours the employee has worked.

All employers need to ensure that they have an accurate record of their employees' full name, home address, gender, date of birth and NI number. Any employees who have left need to be removed from the system, and new employees added so that the record is always fully up to date.

An initial electronic submission needs to be made to HMRC to check that HMRC have the same details for your employees as you do. This allows any errors to be spotted and rectified with either the employer's records or HMRC records.

When the employee data has been aligned with HMRC, approval can then be given for the employer to use the RTI system.

Every time an employee is paid, an electronic report has to be made to HMRC. So, if your employees are paid weekly, there will be reports made every week, but if they are paid monthly, the reports will only be monthly. If an employer pays an employee, but fails to make the appropriate electronic report, the employer will be penalised. This means that businesses are no longer able to pay 'casual' wages.

When an electronic report has been made, it is not possible to make any changes to these details once the following pay period has been run. If an error has been made, or there is some other reason for needing to change the pay details, this will have to be done in the following pay period. Compliance failures are penalised. To help small employers, those businesses having fewer than 10 employees can use the software on the HMRC website in order to make electronic filings to HMRC.

National Minimum Wage and National Living Wage

You must be at least school leaving age to get the National Minimum Wage and aged 23 to get the National Living Wage. The National Living Wage for those aged 23 and over and the National Minimum Wage for those of at least school leaving age are paid at the following rates from 1 April 2021:

Aged 23 and above	£8.91
Aged 21 to 22 inclusive	£8.36
Aged 18 to 20 inclusive	£6.56
Aged under 18 but above compulsory school leaving age	£4.62

HMRC is likely to ask you to prove that you are paying at least these rates, so you must keep records. Failure may result in fines of up to £5,000 for each offence. For more information, call the Acas Helpline on 0300 123 1100.

Statutory Sick Pay, Statutory Maternity Pay, Statutory Paternity Pay, Statutory Adoption Pay and Shared Parental Pay

The best way of finding the full details of these different types of statutory pay is to visit www.gov.uk.

You can get £96.35 per week Statutory Sick Pay (SSP) if you're too ill to work. It's paid by your employer for up to 28 weeks. You need to qualify for SSP and to have been off work sick for four or more days in a row.

Statutory Maternity Pay (SMP) is paid for up to 39 weeks. You get:

- 90% of your average weekly earnings (before tax) for the first six weeks;
- £151.97 or 90% of your average weekly earnings (whichever is lower) for the next 33 weeks.

SMP is paid in the same way as your wages (e.g. monthly or weekly). Tax and National Insurance will be deducted.

The weekly rate of Statutory Paternity Pay (SPP) is £151.97 or 90% of your average weekly earnings (whichever is lower). It is usually paid while you're on leave. Your employer must confirm the start and end dates for your SPP when you claim.

Statutory Adoption Pay (SAP) is paid at a rate of 90% of your average weekly earnings for the first 6 weeks; and the lower of £151.97 or 90% of your gross weekly earnings for the next 33 weeks.

Shared Parental Pay is paid at the same rate as Statutory Maternity Pay.

The tax-deductible expenses an employee is entitled to claim

If you are an employee, which business expenses are deductible for tax purposes and which are not?

There is a general rule that any business expenses must be incurred wholly, exclusively and necessarily for the purposes of the business.

Clothes

Normally allowed – The cost of replacing, cleaning and repairing protective clothing (e.g. overalls, boots) and functional clothing (e.g. uniforms) necessary for your job and which you are required to provide. The cost of cleaning protective clothing or functional clothing provided by your employer, if cleaning facilities are not provided.

Not allowed – Ordinary clothes you wear for work (e.g. pinstripe suit) which you could wear outside work – even if you never choose to.

Tools, etc.

Normally allowed – The cost of maintaining and repairing tools and instruments which you are required to provide. Claims for the replacement of tools can be made using the Annual Investment Allowance regime, which also covers the purchase of new plant and machinery.

Cost of working at home

Normally allowed – A proportion of lighting, heating, telephone, cleaning, insurance, rent, Council Tax, water rates and mortgage interest, if part of your home is used for business. However, these expenses are only allowed if it's necessary that you carry out your duties at or from home (i.e. if it's an express or implied condition of your employment). If part of your home is used exclusively for work, then this could lead to a Capital Gains Tax liability when you come to sell your home.

If you are required by either law or your employer to work from home then, instead of calculating the above figures, you are entitled to claim £6 per week (£312) even if you have only worked one day at home. You can claim on the government's website by visiting https://www.gov.uk/tax-relief-for-employees/working-at-home.

Stationery, etc.

Normally allowed – The cost of reference books which are necessary for your job and which you are required to provide. The cost of stationery used strictly for your job.

Not allowed – The cost of books you feel you need to do your job properly but which are, in fact, unnecessary, as well as subscriptions to journals to keep up with general news.

Interest

Normally allowed – The interest on loans to buy equipment (e.g. a personal computer) necessary for the job.

Not allowed – The interest on an overdraft or credit card.

Travelling

Normally allowed – Expenses incurred strictly in the course of carrying out the job. See also 'Authorised Mileage Allowance Payments' on page 46. A company car: if you pay for fuel, you can claim a lower rate of mileage payment (See 'Advisory fuel rates' on page 47).

Not allowed – Travel from home to your normal place of work.

Accompanying spouses

Normally allowed – The cost of your husband or wife travelling with you if either has, and uses, a practical qualification directly associated with the trip. Often only a proportion of the cost is allowed.

Hotels and meals

Normally allowed – If you keep up a permanent home, reasonable hotel and meal expenses when travelling in the course of your job. In addition, if you stay away overnight while travelling on business, you can claim £5 for incidental expenses to cover private phone calls, laundry and newspapers (£10 per night if you are outside the UK).

Others

Normally allowed – Pension scheme contributions. Professional subscriptions.

Fixed deductions

Fixed deductions are flat rate expenses for employees to cover the cost of tools, special clothing, etc. not provided by their employer. The amounts are mostly agreed with trade unions and don't preclude further claims, if justified.

HM Revenue & Customs' (HMRC) website at Employment Income Manual 50000 to 70199 contains a lot of information about particular occupations and the expenses that can be claimed for them. For example, nursing staff (which includes midwives of all grades, auxiliaries, students and assistants) can claim £125 per annum laundry allowance, £12 per annum shoe allowance and £6 per annum stocking allowance. (For male nurses this can include socks.)

Employees working from home and their Council Tax banding

If you are an employee, so long as your employer agrees that you can work from home (and whether or not your employer provides you with equipment to carry out such work), you may be entitled to seek a reduction in your Council Tax banding on the ground that the room you use as an office can no longer be used, for example as a bedroom. It would be advisable for you not to hold business meetings at your home, because too many of those might constitute a change of use and cause other problems with your local council.

You may be interested to learn (or, more accurately, you should be warned) that one local council, having reduced the Council Tax banding on such a house, sought to impose business rates on the part of the house used for business purposes. However, it failed in its endeavours and the local valuation office decided not to proceed with the case.

Also, using part of your main residence exclusively for business purposes may jeopardise your eligibility for Principal Private Residence relief, and may create a liability to Capital Gains Tax when you come to sell it.

The Working Time Directive

The Working Time Regulations regulate working hours. The rules cover all workers, full-time and part-time, regardless of the size of firm for which they work and including domestic servants. They extend to quite a few who, for tax purposes, would be counted as self-employed, such as freelancers. The Regulations provide that:

1. workers don't work more than 48 hours a week;
2. night workers don't work more than eight hours a night and are offered regular health assessments;
3. workers have a rest period of 11 consecutive hours between each working day;
4. workers have an in-work rest break of 20 minutes when working more than six hours;
5. workers have at least 5.6 weeks' paid leave each year (including bank holidays).

Only in the case of the 48-hour week may individual workers choose to agree to ignore the regulations and work more than 48 hours. If they do, the agreement must be in writing and must allow the worker to bring the agreement to an end.

There are a number of other flexibilities and a lot of detailed definitions. If you would like to learn more, you can obtain information from ACAS or the Department for Business, Energy & Industrial Strategy.

Holiday pay

Holiday pay is not really a tax matter but it can be dealt with under this section. Holiday pay would normally be specified in a contract of employment and all employees should be issued with a contract of employment by their employer. However, whether holiday pay is paid under a contract or under any other arrangement, it forms part of gross pay and is treated exactly the same as any other pay.

Directors and tax

If you are a company director and your company pays you wages, salary, bonus or commission, you must apply the PAYE procedures.

The Income Tax aspect is calculated in exactly the same way as for an employee, but there is a very important difference in the calculation of the National Insurance contributions. If you are a director, at 6 April you need to use the 'annual earnings period' calculation and if you became a director during the year you must use the 'pro-rata annual earnings period'. It's also possible for HMRC to direct that you use the 'annual earnings period' for certain employees (e.g. for the spouse of a director who gets paid an annual bonus).

Providing benefits for employees

Any benefits provided for employees must, in the first instance, be regarded as taxable and liable to be reported to HMRC. The time limit for submitting Forms P11D (Expenses and Benefits) and P11D(b) (Return of Class1A National Insurance contributions due) to the Tax Office is 6 July following the tax year end.

The Class 1A National Insurance (NI) Contribution liability on the employer for any benefits made available to employees is calculated using the P11D information and payment must be made by 22 July (19 July if you pay by cheque). You don't need to submit a P11D for an employee if you're paying tax on all their benefits through your payroll. But you will still need to submit a P11D(b), so you can pay any Class 1A NI Contributions you owe. You can deduct and pay tax on most employee expenses through your payroll as long as you've registered with HMRC before the start of the tax year.

If you provide a trivial benefit to your employees, it is exempt from tax as employment income if all the following conditions are satisfied:

- the cost of providing the benefit does not exceed £50;
- the benefit is not cash or a cash voucher;
- the employee is not entitled to the benefit as part of any contractual obligation;
- the benefit is not provided in recognition of particular services performed by the employee as part of their employment duties.

If your company is a close company (a family company) and the benefit is provided to a director or other office holder of the company (or member of their family or household) the exemption is capped at a total of £300 in the tax year.

Authorised Mileage Allowance Payments

Where an employee uses his own vehicle for company purposes, he will obviously look to his employer for reimbursement for his expenses. These are now repaid using the Authorised Mileage Allowance Payment (AMAP) rates, which show the maximum mileage rate that can be paid tax free.

The rates are shown in the table below and are fairly self-explanatory, but the following illustration may help.

If an employee with his own car (of whatever engine size) on which he personally pays all the expenses were to do a total of 15,000 miles in a tax year on company business, he could be paid 45p per mile for the first 10,000 miles (£4,500) and 25p per mile for the next 5,000 miles (£1,250). In total, he could be paid £5,750 tax free.

There is no requirement to show payments on an employee's Form P11D if payments are within AMAP limits. If the employer pays over the limit, the excess must be declared on the P11D.

The employer should require the completion of an expense form to back up the claim that the mileage was for business purposes.

The rules are:

Authorised Mileage Allowance Payments rates

Business mileage	Any size of Engine
Up to 10,000 miles	45p
Excess over 10,000 miles	25p

Advisory fuel rates

Where an employee provides the fuel for business travel in a company car, he will look to his employer for reimbursement of this expense. HMRC has published advisory fuel rates as follows:

Hybrid cars are treated as either petrol or diesel cars for this purpose. The rate for electric cars is 4p per mile. These rates are reviewed quarterly.

Tax on motor cars provided by an employer

This refers to tax payable by drivers of company cars. It should only concern you if you drive a company car or if you are a director of a company which provides company cars to its employees. This doesn't concern anyone who is self-employed.

In effect, Income Tax payable is assessed on a multiple of the level of CO_2 emitted and the list price of a new car.

So the more the CO_2 and the more expensive the car, the higher the tax bill. Company car drivers of small, environmentally friendly cars get the best deal.

Every case should be judged on its merits, so look before you leap. Your company should be able to assist you with transfer of ownership, arranging favourable terms of purchase and/or finance.

Tax on employees' vans

If you are an employee and are provided with a company van you have to pay tax on it if you make private use of it. If you have the van mainly for work journeys and the only private use is commuting, there is no tax to pay. If there is other private use, tax is payable unless this private use is insignificant. HMRC states that:

Private use is insignificant if:

- it is very much the exception to the normal use;
- it is intermittent and irregular; and
- it lasts only for short periods of time on odd occasions during the year.

Examples of insignificant use include an employee who:

- takes an old mattress or other rubbish to the tip once or twice a year;

- regularly makes a slight detour to drop off a child at school or stops at a newsagent on the way to work; calls at the dentist on the way home from work.

Examples of use which is not insignificant include an employee who:

- regularly uses the van to do the supermarket shopping;
- takes the van away on a week's holiday;
- uses the van outside of work for social activities.

The car benefit charges based on CO_2 emissions for 2021/22

CO_2 emissions in grams per kilometre	Tax is based on the following percentage of the list price of the car first registered before 6th April 2021*
	%
0	1
1-50	This depends on their electric range in miles and varies between 1 and 13%
51-54	14
55-59	15
60-64	16
65-69	17
70-74	18
75-79	19
80-84	20
85-89	21
90-94	22
95-99	23
100-104	24
104-109	25
110-114	26
115-119	27
120-124	28
125-129	29
130-134	30
136-139	31

140-144	32
145-149	33
150-154	34
155-159	35
160-164	36
165 and over	37

*Diesels pay a 4% surcharge on all engine sizes, with a maximum payable of 37%. Cars that meet the Real Driving Emissions Step 2 standard are exempt from the diesel supplement.

Fuel benefit charges

Where an employer pays for the car's private fuel, the taxable benefit is the appropriate percentage from the above table applied to a universal sum of £24,600.

Exemption from tax for travel and subsistence payments

Businesses do not have to pay tax and NIC on paid or reimbursed expenses payments or put them on a P11D. This exemption is subject to the condition that the business satisfies itself that the employee would be entitled to full tax relief on that payment or benefit.

The main types of expense to which the exemption applies are:

- Travel and subsistence expenses
- Fees and subscriptions
- Business entertainment expenses

All other non-allowable expenses are reportable on a P11D and/or subject to PAYE (and possibly NIC). Employees are still able to claim tax relief in respect of unreimbursed business expenses.

Auto-enrolment

Automatic enrolment in a workplace pension. As a strategy to encourage employees to save for their retirement, the government requires that employers provide access to a pension scheme and automatically enrol all eligible employees into it. Once enrolled, employees can opt out; however, the employer has a duty to automatically enrol them back in at regular intervals.

The scheme dictates that both employer and employee must contribute a minimum percentage of the employee's salary into the pension scheme. The employee's minimum is 5% and the employer's minimum is 3%. If you earn more than £6,240 but less than £10,000 in your job, you won't be automatically enrolled but you can ask to join. If you do, your employer also has to contribute.

If you earn £10,000 or more, then you will be automatically enrolled and you will pay contributions on your salary between £6,240 and the amount of your salary, and so will your employer. The upper limit is £50,000 after which neither of you has to pay.

So, for example, if you earn £20,000 in 2021/22, you will pay £20,000 − £6,240 = £13,760 x 5% = £688.00 and your employer will pay £13,760 x 3% = £412.80. You will get tax relief of 20% on your contributions so the net cost to you will be £688.00 − 20% = £550.40.

Providing shares and share options for employees

Under a Share Incentive Plan, employees may allocate part of their salary to shares in their employer company ('partnership shares') without paying tax or National Insurance contributions, nor are employers' National Insurance contributions payable. Employers may also give free shares to employees, including extra free shares for employees who have partnership shares ('matching shares'), and the cost of the shares and of running the scheme are tax deductible. There are maximum limits of £1,800 worth of partnership shares per year and £3,600 worth of free shares per year, although employers may set lower limits.

If the employee takes shares out of the scheme within five years, he is taxed on them. If the shares remain in the scheme for five years or more, they are free of tax and National Insurance contributions when they are withdrawn.

Under a 'Save As You Earn' (SAYE) scheme, contributions of between £5 and £500 per month are paid under a SAYE contract with a building society or bank. At the end of your savings contract (three or five years) you can use the savings to buy shares. The tax advantages are:

• the interest and any bonus at the end of the scheme are tax free; and

- you don't pay tax or National Insurance contributions on the difference between what you pay for the shares and what they are worth.

Under a Company Share Option Plan, you have the option to buy up to £30,000-worth of shares at a fixed price. You won't pay tax or National Insurance contributions on the difference between what you pay for the shares and what they're actually worth. But you may have to pay Capital Gains Tax if you sell the shares.

Schemes for providing shares for employees

The different approved schemes are:

- Share Incentive Plans (SIP): Under this scheme:
  - Employers can give up to £3,600 worth of shares to each employee.
  - Employees can buy up to £1,800 worth of shares and, under such circumstances, employers can reward the purchasers with two free shares for each share purchased.
- Save as You Earn (SAYE):
  - Participants can save up to £500 per month to acquire shares at the end of a three- or five-year period.
- Enterprise Management Incentive (EMI):
  - Companies with gross assets not exceeding £30 million can grant tax and National Insurance Contribution-advantaged share options worth up to £250,000 to any number of employees who work more than 25 hours per week in the business, subject to a total value of £3 million.
- Company Share Option Plans (CSOP):
  - Up to £30,000 of options each can be granted to any number of employees with tax and National Insurance Contribution advantages.
- Schemes outside HMRC's approved range of schemes:
  - These will suffer tax and National Insurance contributions.

Needless to say, professional advice must be sought. For example, shares must not be issued at less than market value. In the case of unapproved schemes, the company makes up its own rules. For these, there is even more need for professional advice because if things go wrong, it can be both embarrassing and expensive.

National Insurance payable on employees' benefits

If you are an employer and you complete Form P11D for any of your employees, it's likely that there will be a Class 1A National Insurance liability arising on the benefits.

The amount of Class 1A National Insurance contributions payable is calculated by reference to the value of the benefits provided and the application of the Class 1A percentage rate in force, currently 13.8 per cent. Calculation of the Class 1A National Insurance Contribution liability will be possible from the information contained in the P11D Form. Payment of the Class 1A National Insurance contributions will be due by 22 July (19 July if you pay by cheque) following the end of the year in question, i.e. 22 July 2022 for 2021/22.

Reading HMRC's guide for employers CWG5, Class 1A contributions on benefits in kind, termination payments and sporting testimonial payments, is recommended and this also contains details of further sources of information.

Employers' and employees' duties at the end of the tax year

Employers

All employers must provide their employees with a P60 End of Year Certificate for the year and also a P11D Expenses and Benefits form as appropriate. The employer must also ensure that all payments of PAYE tax and National Insurance contributions have been paid over to HMRC and any Class 1A National Insurance contributions due for the year will subsequently be payable. The deadlines for these various items are as follows:

Month 12 payment to HMRC to avoid interest	22 April (19 April if you pay by cheque)
Providing the P60 to your employee	31 May
Submitting Forms P11D and P11D(b) to the Tax Office	6 July
Making the Class 1A National Insurance contributions payment to HMRC	22 July (19 July if you pay by cheque)

Employee

You should keep your P60 in a safe place. You should keep evidence of any income that you have received during the year and any tax that you have paid. This is not limited to your employment and includes all of your tax affairs.

Charitable giving through the PAYE system

If an employer participates in the Payroll Giving scheme ('Give As You Earn'), an employee can authorise the deduction of whatever sum he chooses from his earnings before tax, for passing on to charities chosen by him, through a charity agency with which the employer has made an arrangement. The employee thus receives full tax relief for the contributions made.

Tax on termination payments for compensation for loss of office

Termination payments and payments in lieu of notice ('PILONs') are both taxable when provided for in the terms and conditions of the employment. Payments of deferred earnings are also taxable under the normal PAYE rules.

Provided that the payment is not caught by the normal PAYE rules, the first £30,000 of a termination payment not provided for in the terms and conditions of the employment is exempt from tax. Any surplus received over and above this is treated as earnings and PAYE applied in the normal way. Statutory redundancy payments are included within the £30,000 exemption.

Payments for death or disability in service are not taxable. Lump sums received under approved pension schemes are also exempt from tax.

Employers are liable to pay Class 1A National Insurance contributions on termination payments they make to their employees in excess of £30,000. All PILONs are both taxable and subject to NICs.

UK tax rules for those employed outside the UK

If your employment abroad is full-time, spans a complete tax year and you actually carry out all your duties abroad, you are normally treated by concession as a non-resident from the date of leaving until the date of return. If you don't attain non-resident status, you will be a UK resident throughout.

There has been a number of tax cases involving residence issues, and the whole area is becoming increasingly complex, with HMRC taking a much tougher line on residence status. It is therefore recommended that professional advice is sought. There is a statutory residence test, more details on which can be found in chapter 13.

Employment Allowance available for certain employers

Eligible employers can reduce the amount of Employers Class 1 NIC they have to pay by up to £4,000. This is a generous allowance which benefits the vast majority of employers.

Businesses, charities and Community Amateur Sports Clubs can claim the allowance. The term 'businesses' includes sole traders, partnerships and companies. There are, however, some exclusions; you cannot claim Employment Allowance if you:

- employ someone for personal, household or domestic affairs e.g. nanny, au pair, housekeeper, gardener, chauffeur, etc;
- already claim the allowance through a connected business;
- are a public authority;
- are the sole director and employee of your own limited company;
- carry out functions either wholly or mainly of a public nature – unless you have charitable status; examples of this are NHS services, GP services, services to the public on behalf of the local council, etc.

There is more information at www.gov.uk/claim-employment-allowance.

Service companies (as defined for IR35) are not able to claim the Employment Allowance in respect of deemed payments of employment income. Please be aware that the term service company does have a very specific meaning, and is not simply a company which provides a service, e.g. accountancy. Employment Allowance is only available to businesses and charities with an employer NIC bill below £100,000.

CHAPTER 5

Pensions and tax

General rules on pension contributions and tax?

1. If you wish, you can save in more than one pension scheme at the same time.

2. There is no limit on the amount of money you can save in a pension scheme or the number of pension schemes you can save in – although there are limits on the amount of tax relief you can get.

3. You will get tax relief on contributions up to 100 per cent of your annual earnings (up to an annual allowance set at £40,000 for 2020/21 and 2021/22).

   For those with earnings over £150,000 per annum, the amount of pension contributions upon which tax relief can be claimed is tapered down from £40,000 to £10,000.

   So if you put a net contribution of £100 into your pension scheme, the government will put in another £25 so that your gross contribution is £125.

4. If you are a higher or additional rate taxpayer, you will get extra tax relief on the gross contribution of £125 (£25 in the case of a 40 per cent taxpayer and £31.25 in the case of a 45 per cent taxpayer).

5. Even if you are not a taxpayer, you can still get tax relief on pension contributions. You can put in up to £2,880 in any one tax year and the government will top this up with another £720 – giving you total pension savings with tax relief of £3,600 per year.

6. The rules about retirement are flexible. You can continue working while drawing your pension, where the scheme rules allow it.

7. If your scheme rules allow, you can take up to 25 per cent of your pension fund as a tax-free lump sum.

8. If your pension pot is more than the 'lifetime allowance' when you come to take your pension, you may be subject to a tax charge at that time. But this will only apply if your total pension savings are in excess of £1,073,100 for 2020/21 and 2021/22.

9. You cannot take a pension before you are 55 (rising to 57 from 2028), although you can retire early due to poor health.

10. You can now access your pension funds without having to purchase an annuity. However, it is strongly recommended that anyone becoming eligible to draw their pension should take professional advice on their options. There are a lot of scammers about and there have been a number of frauds. In some cases, pensioners have lost their entire pension pot. Pension scams can be hard to spot. Scammers can be articulate and financially knowledgeable, with credible-looking websites, testimonials and materials that are hard to distinguish from the real thing. Scammers usually contact people out of the blue via phone, email or text, or even advertise online. Or they may be introduced to you by a friend or family member who is also unknowingly being scammed.

Pension schemes

Over the years of our being in practice, we have discovered that clients save towards their retirement in a number of different ways. Some don't wish to pay into a pension scheme, preferring to invest on their own, through either property or other types of investment. This route doesn't suit everyone and we encourage our clients to make sure that they are fully aware of the associated risks before pursuing such a strategy.

For many, the discipline of saving on a regular basis for their retirement appeals along with the attraction of tax relief on contributions and the virtually tax-free growth that can be enjoyed while their money is invested.

Whichever route our clients take, there are obviously charges to consider. For pensions this could be fees paid to an adviser, while for property purchase it might be legal fees such as Stamp Duty, solicitor's costs, etc.

SIPPs

SIPPs are Self Invested Personal Pensions and they allow individuals direct control over the investments in their pension scheme. They provide maximum flexibility in the timing of contributions into, and benefit payments from, the scheme.

An example of such flexibility is that a SIPP allows for up to 25 per cent of the fund to be withdrawn tax free between the ages of 55 and 75. The balance then can be used to provide income for the rest of the individual's life.

SIPPs also provide an attraction for Inheritance Tax purposes because if the individual dies before retirement, the whole of the value of the SIPP is excluded from the deceased's estate.

There are many assets that can be included in a SIPP but some are specifically excluded (e.g. residential property, works of art, fine wines and vintage cars).

One advantage of a SIPP is the opportunity it provides for investing in smaller companies. Another is that a SIPP can borrow up to 50 per cent of its value.

Some individuals who invest in a SIPP opt for the management to be handled at the discretion of an investment management company. One advantage of this is the clear reporting and administrative package that usually comes with such management.

State pension forecast

If you ring up the Pension Service (tel 0800 731 0175) and give it your National Insurance number, it should be able to send you a forecast of your anticipated state pension at retirement, which it will work out based on your age and contributions.

You can also complete a State Pension Statement request form (BR19), which is available online. A single-tier state pension has been introduced for people who reached pension age on or after April 2016. The full rate is £179.60 per week in 2021/22.

The starting date for payment of the state pension

The pension ages for women have increased and men's and women's state pension ages are now unified. The state pension age has increased for both sexes to 66 in the period November 2018 to October 2020. It then increases to 67. This change is to be implemented between 2026 and 2028.

There are further plans to increase the state pension age to 68, which are scheduled to be implemented between 2037 and 2039.

Deferring the state pension

Whether you have yet to start receiving your state pension or are already receiving it, it is possible to defer payment.

This can be advantageous if you reach pension age but are continuing to work. It may be that claiming your pension would make you liable to higher rates of tax, for example.

If receipt of your pension is deferred, you can gain an increase in your pension of one per cent for every nine weeks of deferral. This works out at about 5.8% per year.

If you put off claiming your pension for at least 12 continuous months, you can choose to receive your pension at the normal rate plus a one-off lump sum. This lump sum is taxable, but you may be able to have it paid in a year when you are liable to lower rates of tax than if you had not deferred it.

As you are forgoing your pension now for additional pension later, there is a strong investment aspect to the decision. It is therefore recommended that you take advice on the matter from an independent financial adviser.

CHAPTER 6

Self-employment and partnerships

Informing the taxman that one is going self-employed or starting a partnership

When you begin self-employment it's very important that somebody (you or your accountant) tells HM Revenue & Customs (HMRC) that you have begun in business, partly so that the correct tax can be paid on time and partly so that the appropriate National Insurance contributions are paid. Anyone beginning self-employment or a partnership must register with HMRC by 5 October of his business's second trading year. Failure to meet this deadline can result in a £100 penalty.

If you've sent a Tax Return before, register online. You'll need your 10-digit unique tax reference (UTR) for this.

If you haven't sent a Return before, register online and you'll get a letter with your UTR and be enrolled for the self-assessment online service at the same time.

If you are a partner in a partnership, there are two forms which you should complete for the tax authorities, SA400 Registering a partnership for Self Assessment and SA401 Registering a partner for Self Assessment (or you can do it online). Self-employment worries can be taken care of (and avoided) if you choose an accountant to handle your accounts and to advise you about the resulting tax liabilities.

The question of trading

It's sometimes difficult to know if an activity is taxable or not. Typical (in other words difficult) questions might be as follows:

- If I earn £300 a year from self-employed activities, does the taxman want to know?
- My daughter, who is still at school, earns £50 a week from singing in local pubs; does the taxman want to know?
- I occasionally do small jobs for people, being paid in cash; will the taxman want to know?

It's always difficult to give the right answer because, while we know that under law if you are earning money the taxman will want to know, even if there is no tax to be paid, there is that famous maxim, which we cover elsewhere in this book, de minimis non curat lex, which means 'the law is not concerned with trifles'.

Trading is earning money from an activity. Trading involves not only the earning of the money but also the expenses in achieving that income. Our advice to clients is: use the template we show in Appendix 3 and see if you have made a taxable sum from the activity. If you have, you should report it. Your conscience will tell you if you should be reporting it.

When an activity is in the grey area of being between non-reportable and reportable, each case has to be taken on its merits and decisions arrived at accordingly. However, in principle, once one is trading (earning money from an activity) proper records should be kept and HMRC should be told.

There is also a trading allowance which provides for a complete exemption from Income Tax if total trading and miscellaneous income in the year is less than £1,000. Not only is there no Income Tax to pay, but there's also no need to register with HMRC or file Tax Returns, provided trading income is below this level (for more details of how this works, see below).

Calculating taxable income from trading

Basically, you have to take your income and deduct from it all your legitimate business-related expenses. You will see the type of expenses that you can claim in Appendix 3 and in more detail below. However, do bear in mind that some expenses, for instance motoring, may well involve an element of private use. You should only claim that element that relates to the business activity against your trading receipts. It may be that you should only claim a third of your motoring costs against your business. Perhaps a quarter of your Council Tax and insurance costs. Whatever it is, if you have any difficulties in deciding, either go and see a local accountant or call the Tax Office to discuss it.

A template to help you prepare your figures for the self-employed part of the Tax Return is provided at Appendix 3.

Allowable expenses

There is a general rule that any business expenses must be incurred wholly and exclusively for the purposes of the business. This means that some expenses will fall foul of the so-called dual purpose rule. For example, if you attend a business conference in Spain and tack a holiday on the end, your trip will have a dual purpose and the expenses won't be allowed. However, according to HMRC, 'in practice some dual purpose expenses include an obvious part which is for the purposes of the business. We usually allow the deduction of a proportion of expenses like that', and they go on to give the example of car or van expenses.

Basic costs and general running expenses

Normally allowed – The cost of goods bought for resale and raw materials used in business. Advertising, delivery charges, heating, lighting, cleaning, rates, telephone. The rent of business premises. Small tools and special clothing. Postage, stationery, relevant books and magazines. Accountants' fees. Bank charges on business accounts. Fees to professional bodies. Security expenditure.

Not allowed – The initial cost of machinery, vehicles, equipment – but you can claim Annual Investment Allowances, and where the limit for this has been exceeded, Capital Allowances, on these and so-called 'integral features'. The cost of buildings – but you can claim Structures and Buildings Allowance on these. Providing for anticipated expenses in the future.

Use of home for work

Normally allowed – The business proportion of telephone calls and line rental, lighting, heating, cleaning, insurance, rent, Council Tax and mortgage interest. Provided you don't use any part of your home exclusively for business purposes, you won't lose your entitlement to private residence relief for Capital Gains Tax.

Wages and salaries

Normally allowed – Wages, salaries, redundancy and leaving payments paid to employees. Pensions for past employees and their dependants. Staff training. Reasonable pay for your spouse, provided he is actually employed.

Not allowed – Your own wages or salary or that of any business partner. Your own drawings.

Tax and National Insurance

Normally allowed – Employer's National Insurance contributions for employees.

Not allowed – Income Tax. Capital Gains Tax. Inheritance Tax. Your own National Insurance contributions.

Entertaining

Normally allowed – Entertainment of own staff (e.g. a Christmas party).

Not allowed – Any other business entertaining.

Pre-trading expenses

Normally allowed – Revenue business expenditure incurred within seven years before starting to trade.

Gifts

Normally allowed – Gifts costing up to £50 a year to each person so long as the gift advertises your business (or things it sells). Gifts (whatever their value) to employees.

Not allowed – Food, drink, tobacco or vouchers for goods given to anyone other than employees.

Travelling

Normally allowed – Hotel and travelling expenses on business trips. Travel between different places of work. The running costs of your own car – whole of cost if used wholly for business, proportion if used privately too.

Not allowed – Travel between home and business. The cost of buying a car or van (but you can claim Capital Allowances).

Leased cars with CO2 emissions of more than 50g/km (110g/km for cars bought before 1 April 2021) will have 15 per cent of the leasing payments disallowed. There is no restriction for cars with CO2 emissions of less than or equal to 50g/km.

Interest payments

Normally allowed – The interest on overdrafts and loans for business purposes.

Not allowed – The interest on capital paid or credited to partners.

Hire purchase

Normally allowed – Interest element of instalments (i.e. not the capital cost).

Not allowed – Capital element of instalments (but you may get Capital Allowances).

Hiring

Normally allowed – Reasonable charge for hire of capital goods, including cars.

Insurance

Normally allowed – Business insurance (e.g. employer's liability, fire and theft, motor, insuring employees' lives).

Not allowed – Your own life insurance.

Trade marks

Normally allowed – Fees paid to register a trademark, design or patent.

Not allowed – The cost of buying a patent from someone else (but you may get Capital Allowances).

Legal costs

Normally allowed – The costs of recovering debts, defending business rights, preparing service agreements, appealing against rates, renewing a lease for a period not exceeding 50 years (but not if a premium is paid).

Not allowed – Expenses (including Stamp Duty) for acquiring land, buildings or leases. Fines and other penalties for breaking the law, for example parking/speeding fines.

Repairs

Normally allowed – Normal repairs and maintenance to premises or equipment.

Not allowed – The cost of additions, alterations, improvements (but you may get Capital Allowances).

Debts

Normally allowed – Specific provisions for debts and debts written off.

Not allowed – General reserve for bad or doubtful debts.

Subscriptions

Normally allowed – Payments which secure benefits for your business or staff. Payments to societies that have arrangements with HMRC (in some cases only a proportion).

Not allowed – Payments to political parties, churches and charities (but gifts to local churches and charities will be allowed if it can be shown that they were made wholly and exclusively for the purposes of the business).

Travelling and subsistence expenses and tax

Expenses	Employer	Self-employed	Can VAT be reclaimed?
	Where expenses are incurred by the employer, whether a self-employed trader or partnership	Where a self-employed trader incurs these on his own behalf	
Entertaining own staff	Allowable	Allowable	Yes*
Business travel between place of business and customers, etc. (but not home)	Allowable	Allowable	Yes
Hotel bills, etc.	Allowable	Allowable	Yes
Drinks and meals away from home:			
1. Working / Selling	Allowable	Allowable	Yes*
2. On training course	Allowable	Allowable	Yes*
3. Buying, trips, etc.	Allowable	Allowable	Yes*
Entertaining business clients	Not allowable	Not allowable	No
Car parking	Allowable	Allowable	Yes
Trade show expenses	Allowable	Allowable	Yes
Fuel	Allowable	Allowable (Business Proportion only)	Yes**

* But not if there is any measurable degree of business entertainment.

** But if the input VAT is reclaimed, remember to include the scale charge in your output tax on the VAT Return (self-employed only).

Allowable expenses for the self-employed who are working from home

You can claim a proportion of your mortgage interest or rent, Council Tax, insurance, light and heat, water, cleaning, and other costs. One way of doing this is to add up all your costs and then multiply this by the number of rooms you use for business and divide the result by the total number of reception and bedrooms in the property. If you are an owner occupier, provided you don't use any part of your property exclusively for business purposes, you won't lose your entitlement to private residence relief for Capital Gains Tax. You can also claim the business proportion of telephone calls and line rental.

Another method is the simplified way of working all this out. You can calculate your allowable expenses using a flat rate, based on the hours you work from home each month. The flat rate doesn't include telephone or internet expenses; you can still claim the business proportion of these bills by working out the actual costs.

You can only use simplified expenses if you work for 25 hours or more a month from home.

Hours of business use per month	Flat rate per month
25 to 50	£10
51 to 100	£18
101 and more	£26

So, the maximum you can claim using this method is: £26 x 12 = £312.

Wages or Salary paid to oneself

You cannot claim for a wage or salary paid to yourself. If you were to pay yourself a salary out of your self-employment or partnership income, you would have to include the salary as employment income elsewhere on your Tax Return and thereby you would achieve nothing. However, under this section you could also consider whether to pay your spouse or partner a wage etc. If he or she plays a part in the business and has no other income, then there might well be tax to save by paying him or her for the work done.

Trading stock

If you are running a business that involves the buying and selling of items of stock, at the end of your trading year you have to add up the cost of any unsold stock and deduct it from the cost of your purchases acquired during the year. The reason for this is that those stocks are going to be sold in the following accounting period and therefore you only take advantage of the tax relief that goes with buying those stocks in the year or period in which they are sold. In other words any stocks that you deduct from the cost of your purchases at the end of your trading period should be added to the costs that you incur in the following year, so that you claim the deduction in the correct year. If you think that your stock may not sell for what you paid for it or it's slow moving, you can write it down to what is called 'net realisable value'.

Work in progress

If you have been working on a long contract, the duration of which straddles the end of your accounting period, you are likely to have incurred costs in terms of labour and materials at the end of your year which relate to that contract and which you have not been paid for. Accordingly, you should value those materials, as well as those hours and, as with stocks, carry the sum forward to the following year so as to take advantage of those costs in the year in which you bill your customer for the work.

Do remember that, in assessing the value of work in progress, if you are a partner or a sole proprietor in a business, you don't need to include your own time. However, you do need to include materials.

If you have reached a point where you are entitled to be paid for the work done, then instead of carrying forward that work in progress at cost, an appropriate amount of income should be included at selling price. This is a complicated area and we do recommend that you take advice from either HMRC or a Chartered Accountant.

Debtors

Debtors are your customers who owe you money. Even though you have not been paid, these amounts must be included in your sales and in your balance sheet. If any of them have subsequently proved to be bad or look doubtful (i.e. you are not going to be paid or you may not be paid), you can claim as an expense a figure relating specifically to the ones that are not going to be, or may not be, paid.

Come the next accounting period, and when that cash comes in, you don't pay tax on that money, because it has already been taxed in the previous year.

Creditors

Creditors are like debtors but the other way round: they are the suppliers to whom you owe money. You are allowed to include amounts owing in your accounts, and get the tax relief for them in the year to which they relate. However, when you come to pay them in the following year, you won't be entitled to tax relief in that year because you have already got the tax relief in the previous year.

Capital Allowances

You cannot claim the depreciation on fixed assets charged in your accounts as a tax deduction. Instead, you may claim, and in a prescribed way, HMRC's own version of depreciation, which it calls 'Capital Allowances'. There are three types of Capital Allowance: First Year Allowance, Annual Investment Allowance and Writing Down Allowance.

First Year Allowances

If you buy an asset that qualifies for First Year Allowance (FYA), you can deduct the full cost from your profits before tax. You can claim an enhanced capital allowance (a type of FYA), for the following energy and water-efficient equipment:

- some cars with low CO_2 emissions;
- energy-saving equipment that's on the energy technology product list, e.g. certain motors;
- water-saving equipment that's on the water-efficient technologies product list, e.g. meters, efficient toilets and taps;
- plant and machinery for gas refuelling stations, e.g. storage tanks and pumps;
- gas, biogas and hydrogen refuelling equipment; and
- new, zero-emission goods vehicles.

Annual Investment Allowance

You can deduct the full value of an item that qualifies for annual investment allowance (AIA) from your profits before tax. You can claim AIA on most plant and machinery up to £1,000,000 until 31st December 2021. You can't claim AIA on:

- cars;
- items you owned for another reason before you started using them in your business;
- items given to you or your business.

You should claim Writing Down Allowances instead.

Writing Down Allowances

Once you have claimed any FYA and AIA and if you still have capital expenditure on which you have not claimed so far, you can claim writing down allowances (WDA). WDA is when you deduct a percentage of the value of an item from your profits each year.

The percentage you deduct depends on the item. For business cars the rate depends on their CO_2 emissions.

The following table shows what you can claim FYA and WDA on:

	First Year Allowance % that can be claimed by any business	Writing Down Allowance % that can be claimed
Plant	Nil	18%
Machinery	Nil	18%
Vans	Nil	18%
Patents	Nil	18%
Know-how (a kind of intellectual property)	Nil	25%
Information and Communications Technology	Nil	18%
Computers	Nil	Nil
Digital TV	Nil	18%
Websites	18%	18%

Energy-saving, and water-saving plant and machinery[1]	100%	Nil
Cars	Nil	18%[2]
Cars with low CO_2 emissions (less than 50 g/km)	100%	Nil
Special rate assets[3]	Nil	6%

[1] See the Energy Technology List at https://www.gov.uk/guidance/energy-technology-list for details.

[2] For new cars with CO_2 emissions above 110g/km, the rate is 6%. For cars with CO_2 emissions more than 50g/km and less than or equal to 110g/km, the rate is 18%.

[3] This includes long life assets, integral features, certain thermal insulation and some cars.

For more information on capital allowances, please refer to chapter 12, Corporation Tax.

Allowances for long life assets

Long life assets are items of plant or machinery which are expected to last at least 25 years. The writing down allowance for them is six per cent. A new 'pool' is created to include long life assets and integral features. Integral features include electrical systems, cold water systems, heating systems, air conditioning, lifts and escalators.

Farmers

There are two specific ways in which farmers get special tax treatment:

1. **The herd basis.** The principle of the herd basis is that, because a herd, or a flock for that matter, consists of breeding animals (cows, bulls, rams, ewes), instead of treating these as animals that you will ultimately sell as meat, you treat them as capital assets and not as a revenue item. This book on tax is not the place to describe this particular feature, but the effect of claiming the herd basis at a time of rising animal values is that, when you come to sell those animals (perhaps retire), a substantial part of the sale proceeds won't be subject to tax.

   How should farmers value their stock? Farm stocks and farm animals that are not part of a herd or flock should be valued at the lower of cost or net realisable value. In a number of cases 'cost' will be easy to calculate, but what about animals that have grown considerably since they were bought, animals that have been home bred and crops? For such stocks where it's just not possible to calculate an appropriate 'cost' figure, HMRC allows farmers to use a percentage of market value at the valuation date. These are:

- Cattle: 60%
- Sheep and pigs: 75%
- Deadstock: 75%

2. **Averaging.** Because farm results can fluctuate, farmers are able to claim the averaging of profits of any five-year period of assessment, provided they do so within broadly 22 months of the end of the fifth year. As with the herd basis, the rules can be quite complicated, but the effect of claiming for averaging is that you can collectively pay less tax than you would if you had high profits attracting higher rates of tax in one year and lower profits in the adjacent year.

Lloyd's insurance underwriters

Yes, there is special treatment for Lloyd's underwriters. It's such a complicated set of rules, allowances and regulations that our advice is to say, as succinctly as possible, go to a specialist adviser who deals with Lloyd's underwriters.

Subcontractors

The Construction Industry Scheme (CIS) works as follows:

1. There is a verification process which determines whether subcontractors should be paid gross or net. Subcontractors applying for registration have to prove their identity to HMRC, who then register the applicant for payment under deduction at the 20 per cent rate. Subcontractors who are not verified will suffer a 30% tax deduction by the contractor. Those registering for gross payment have to satisfy three further tests:

   a) **Turnover test:** HMRC will look at your business turnover from construction work for the 12 months before you apply for gross payment status. Ignoring VAT and the cost of materials, your construction turnover must be at least:

- £30,000 if you are a sole trader;
- £30,000 for each partner in a partnership, or at least £100,000 for the whole partnership;
- £30,000 for each director of a company, or at least £200,000 for the whole company.

If your company is controlled by five people or fewer, you must have an annual turnover of £30,000 per each of them.

b) **Compliance test:** You and any directors or partners in the business, or beneficial shareholders (where the company is controlled by five or fewer people) must have submitted all Tax Returns and paid all tax due on time in the 12 months before your application. If HMRC has asked for any information about your tax affairs in that period, you will need to have given it to them.

You are allowed a few lapses or late payments in the 12 months and HMRC will ignore any, or all, of the following failures:

- three late submissions of the CIS contractor monthly return, including 'nil' returns – up to 28 days late;
- three late payments of CIS/PAYE deductions – up to 14 days late;
- one late payment of self-assessment tax – up to 28 days late;
- any employer's end of year return made late;
- any late payment of Corporation Tax – up to 28 days late, including where any shortfall in the payment has incurred an interest charge, but no penalty;
- any self-assessment return made late;
- any payment not made by the due date, where it is less than £100.

c) **Business test:** You must show HMRC that your business carries out construction work – or provides labour for construction work – in the UK, and that it is run largely through a bank account.

2. Contractors have to make monthly returns and provide monthly statements of amounts paid. Contractors have 14 days to send in the returns and make payment (17 days if the payment is made electronically) and nil returns have to be submitted.

3. The contractor has to declare that it considers the subcontractor to be self-employed. This is always a difficult area and the questionnaire on pages 35-37 may be a useful starting point.

4. There is a 30 per cent rate of deduction which is to be used for those who are not registered.

Contractors would be well advised to have suitable software in place to cope with the monthly returns and paperwork. Penalties range from £100 up to £3,000.

Royalties

If you are an author or composer by profession, then your receipts are taxed as part of your professional earnings and you are able to deduct more expenses than otherwise would be the case. In principle, you pay tax in the year in which the royalties are received, but there are rules for spreading royalty receipts over a number of years and, should you fall within this case, we strongly advise you to seek professional advice.

Tax exemption for small amounts of income

There are two exemptions for trading and property income respectively.

Trading allowance

The trading allowance provides for a complete exemption from Income Tax if total trading and miscellaneous income in the year is less than £1,000. Not only is there no Income Tax to pay, but there's also no need to register with HMRC or file Tax Returns, provided trading income is below this level. The £1,000 threshold applies to income, not profits, and there are some complications and exceptions to be aware of.

Individuals who qualify for full exemption will need to monitor their income levels year-on-year; if their income goes above £1,000, they will be subject to self-assessment.

Where trading income exceeds £1,000, the legislation allows for so-called partial relief. Effectively, individuals can choose to either:

- deduct their actual business expenses from trading income in the usual way; or
- elect instead for the £1,000 trading allowance as a deduction from income.

If you claim partial relief, you cannot deduct any other expenses, just the £1,000 allowance.

Property Allowance

The Property Allowance is a tax exemption of up to £1,000 a year for individuals with income from property. If you own a property jointly with others, you're each eligible for the £1,000 allowance against your share of the gross rental income. If your annual gross income is £1,000 or less, you won't need to tell HMRC. If it's higher, you'll need to declare your property income. You can't claim the allowance on income from letting your own home under the Rent a Room Scheme.

Losses and how to claim relief for them

Trading losses may be:

1. relieved against income or gains of the same year;
2. relieved against income or gains of the previous year;
3. carried forward against future profits of the same trade.

In the case of both points 1 and 2, you must claim the full loss, up to the total income for that year. For individuals carrying on a trade in a non-active capacity, i.e. spending on average less than ten hours per week on the commercial activities of the trade, there is an annual limit of £25,000 for losses which can be set against other income in the year.

In the case of point 3 above, if the accounts of a self-employed business or partnership are prepared on the cash basis (in general that means that no balance sheet has been prepared) then trading losses can only be carried forward and relieved against future trading profits.

The amount of Income Tax relief that an individual may claim for deduction from their total income in a tax year is restricted. The limit is the greater of £50,000 or 25 per cent of the individual's adjusted total income.

Reliefs subject to the limit include:

- Trade loss relief against total income.
- Early trade losses relief.
- Post-cessation trade relief.

The limit does not apply to relief in the following circumstances:

- To deductions of trade loss relief, or post-cessation trade relief, made from profits of the same trade.
- To the extent that the trade loss relief is attributable to deductions of overlap relief.

Please note that there is a temporary additional relief for claiming losses called Extended Loss Carry Back. Please refer to page 113 for further details.

Farm losses

Because a number of wealthy people used to claim the substantial losses they made through their farming activities against their other substantial income, HMRC said that it would limit the number of years for which someone in this category could go on claiming farming losses.

For a new farming business which is starting up, you can claim loss relief for six years. For an ongoing farming business, i.e. not a commencement scenario, the answer is five. A loss in the sixth tax year of a consecutive run of farming losses can only be relieved against later profits of the same trade. Once you have made a farming profit then the five-year sequence starts again.

The figure of loss or profit is arrived at before claiming Capital Allowances.

HMRC allows stud farms to incur losses for 11 years.

Class 4 National Insurance

If you are trading and your profits exceed £9,568, you have to pay nine per cent Class 4 National Insurance contributions on the figure of your profits above £9,568 with an annual upper earnings limit of £50,270. Above this upper earnings limit, you have to pay two per cent on all profits above this figure.

Partnership income

A partnership is a formal business arrangement entered into by two or more people whereby the profits and losses of a business are shared in agreed proportions.

In order for HMRC to be happy that a partnership exists, it may want to see a number of the following items before it will agree to tax the business as a partnership:

- A partnership deed
- The names of partners on bank statements
- The names of partners on business letterheadings and other printed stationery

- Some sort of evidence that the parties agreed that there should be a formal partnership between them

There are restrictions on losses made by 'non-active' partners in the first four years. If the loss is claimed against other income or gains, it is restricted to the capital contribution made, unless the partner works more than ten hours a week for the partnership.

Partnership with a spouse or civil partner?

If your spouse or civil partner makes a genuine contribution to the business either by way of capital contribution or by way of time worked for it, then there is no reason why they should not become a partner. It is important for any partnership to be a real one (and not simply a tax dodge – because those don't work). Due recognition must be given to the fact that there are certain legal obligations which go with being a partner.

Obvious cases where husband and wife partnerships should exist are where they both share equally in the work and it's only right and proper that they should be partners. However, there are some disadvantages:

- both partners become jointly and severally liable for the partnership debts and this can put the family home at risk;
- in the case of divorce, the 'busting' of the partnership can result in the complete cessation of the business.

Where there is a bona fide husband/wife partnership, the following documentation should be available to prove its existence to HMRC:

1. There should be a letter issued to all customers of the business stating the appointment of a new partner and the date of the appointment.
2. There should be a written partnership agreement.
3. The names of the partners should appear on the letterheads and invoices, etc. of the business.
4. The names of the partners should appear on the business bank account.
5. The names of the partners should appear in the advertising and promotional literature.
6. If the business is VAT-registered, then it should be registered as a partnership with both the names of the partners on the VAT Return.
7. There should be a Notice of Particulars of Ownership displayed at the business's main centre so that any casual caller will see that there is a partnership in existence.

Partnership agreement

Our advice to any partners is that there should be a written partnership agreement so that, if anything should happen to one of the partners, or they should fall out, there is a legal agreement entered into at the start which establishes how the partnership should be dissolved and how the assets and liabilities should be allocated.

Limited liability partnerships

The Limited Liability Partnerships Act 2000 allows organisations the flexibility to enjoy limited liability while organising themselves (sharing profits, etc.) as partnerships. The limited liability partnership (LLP) is a separate legal entity. It's governed by an agreement between the members (the incorporation document). It is required to file at Companies House similar information to that required of companies, but it is taxed as a partnership.

We are ambivalent about LLPs because we regard the limitation of liability as being more theoretical than real. When companies fail, the directors often have to pay up on previously given personal guarantees and, if the company has failed through any negligence on the part of the directors, then they can be sued as private individuals. The same can apply to limited liability partners.

In principle, we think LLPs are a good thing, but in practice we don't think they have made much difference to anybody. Not that many LLPs have been registered and those that have are mainly large professional firms. There can be occasions when an LLP structure, rather than a limited company, is more suited to a new business; an example of this is when losses are expected to be made in the first year or two, and the partners have other income against which these losses can be relieved.

Taxation of partnerships

Partnerships have their own Tax Return. The accounts are entered into the relevant boxes on the Partnership Tax Return and the profits or losses are allocated between the partners in the agreed proportions.

In addition, the partnership must prepare individual sheets called either 'Partnership (Short)' or 'Partnership (Long)' depending on the nature of the income that the partnership earns, and these individual sheets are handed to the partners themselves so that they can include their share of the partnership's profits and losses in their own individual personal Tax Returns.

In other words, partnerships don't pay tax. It's the partners who pay tax on their share of the profits or claim relief for their share of the losses.

Partnership capital gains

If a partnership makes a capital gain, the proceeds of sale are included on the Partnership Tax Return. The chargeable gain is computed and then each partner's share is added to his or her personal Tax Return, so that each pays Capital Gains Tax on his or her share of the gain.

Change of partners

Partnership changes are notified to HMRC by way of the Partnership Tax Return. When partners change, the apportionment of profits or losses is likely also to change. When the agreed profit or loss for the year in question is allocated to the varying partners (whether static, incoming or outgoing), that share is shown clearly on the Partnership Tax Return and the individual partners themselves pay the tax that their share attracts.

Accounting records – how long to keep?

There is a legal requirement to keep accounting records for six years from the Tax Return filing deadline to which the accounts relate.

HM Revenue & Customs inquiries

HM Revenue & Customs (HMRC) is entitled to investigate a taxpayer's affairs for one of three reasons: either:

1. it thinks a minor point is wrong and needs to be corrected (an 'aspect' enquiry); or
2. it doesn't like the look of the accounts and suspects that there may be something fundamentally wrong (a 'full' enquiry); or
3. the nasty bit, a Tax Return may be selected at random. But few, if any, are so selected these days. HMRC's approach is risk based. Businesses that handle a lot of cash are far more likely to be selected than those that do not.

HMRC is gathering a lot of data on an increasing range of different businesses. This will allow them to ascertain what the 'normal' gross profit rates are for a given type of business. Therefore, when a business submits accounts and the gross profit percentage is outside of HMRC's expected range, this could trigger an enquiry.

CHAPTER 7

Income from land and property

Property income and tax

The rules for the taxation of rental and other property income are similar to the rules for the taxation of trading income. So, you take the gross rental and other income for the year ended 5 April and deduct from it any expenses which relate wholly and exclusively to the property business. HMRC list the following possible items:

- interest on a mortgage to buy the property (but see the restrictive rules for buy-to-let landlords below)
- general maintenance and repairs to the property, but not improvements (such as replacing a laminate kitchen worktop with a granite worktop)
- water rates, council tax, gas and electricity
- insurance, such as landlords' policies for buildings, contents and public liability
- costs of services, including the wages of gardeners and cleaners
- letting agent fees and management fees
- legal fees for lets of a year or less, or for renewing a lease for less than 50 years
- accountant's fees
- rents (if you're sub-letting), ground rents and service charges
- direct costs such as phone calls, stationery and advertising for new tenants
- vehicle running costs (only the proportion used for your rental business) including mileage rate deductions for business motoring costs.

The net profit, i.e. rental income less expenses, is the amount on which you pay tax.

Losses from land and property

There is a difference between the tax treatment of a land and property loss and a trading loss. Losses from land and property businesses can only be carried forward and set against profits in subsequent years from land and property. If you have land or property overseas, any losses made can only be relieved against future profits from that same property.

Furnished lettings and furnished holiday lettings

Furnished lettings

If you receive income from furnished lettings, it's taxed under the property income rules.

If you provide laundry, meals, domestic help, etc. for your tenants, then you may be able to claim that you are running a self-employed business – as you usually can if you are providing holiday lettings (see below). The advantage of running your property enterprise as a trading business means that there are usually more expenses you can claim against Income Tax and, in addition, you may be able to claim Business Asset Disposal Relief for Capital Gains Tax and Business Property Relief for Inheritance Tax purposes. However, this does depend to a large extent on the amount of services you are providing.

Furnished holiday lettings

The definition of furnished holiday lettings is as follows:

- The accommodation must be available for holiday lets for at least 210 days per year.
- The accommodation must be commercially let for at least 105 days in the year.
- No let is to exceed 155 days.

There are special rules for the years of commencement and cessation. The income is treated as earned income (a trade) attracting Capital Gains Tax Rollover Relief and Business Asset Disposal Relief. Tax-saving ideas worth thinking about:

- Rollover of capital gains on the sale of trading assets into the purchase of holiday accommodation.

- Any gain on the sale of the holiday accommodation may eventually attract Capital Gains Tax at only ten per cent. (See page 97.)
- You can claim capital allowances on furniture and equipment.

However:

- If you buy the accommodation with a substantial mortgage, HM Revenue & Customs (HMRC) may regard your motives as not being commercial.
- Don't forget about the VAT consequences, if you are VAT-registered.
- Any losses that are incurred can only be carried forward and set against profits of the same holiday business, not other categories of income or lettings. Furnished holiday lettings within the UK, compared to any outside the UK but in the European Economic Area, say in France, are also separated for loss purposes.

Rent-a-room relief

If you let a room in your house or flat and you are an owner-occupier, or a tenant who is subletting, the first £7,500 of any income is tax free, i.e. a rent of £144.23 per week is tax free. If the rent is higher than £7,500, you either elect to pay tax on the surplus above £7,500 (without relief for expenses) or you can treat the arrangement as being a furnished letting and prepare accounts.

This relief is available whether you rent out just one room to a lodger or you run a bed & breakfast business from your house. Relief is not normally available to people living abroad or in job-related accommodation and letting their home while they are away.

Woodlands and the rules about selling timber

There is no Income Tax charge on woodlands; neither woodland rent nor the sale of timber is taxed. There is no charge to Capital Gains Tax on trees that are standing or felled. In other words, profits on the sale of timber are not taxed at all and losses are not allowable.

Property developers and tax

You may find, perhaps because you are a developer, that you carry out a number of purchases and sales of land and buildings and that, instead of these transactions being treated as falling within the Capital Gains Tax regime, the profits and losses you make are caught under the Income Tax regime. There are some taxpayers who have been badly caught by this and in principle it's quite difficult to give a hard-and-fast rule as to when somebody moves from the Capital Gains Tax regime to the Income Tax regime. However, all may not be lost, because when a capital asset falls within the Income Tax regime, not only are the losses more favourably treated, but also there are usually more expenses that can be claimed as well.

In our opinion, you should seek professional advice if this eventuality comes to pass in your case.

Buy-to-let landlords

Relief on all residential finance costs is restricted to the basic rate of tax.

This relief is given as a basic rate tax reduction. The reduction is the basic rate value (20%) of the lower of:

- **finance costs** - costs not deducted from rental income in the tax year plus any finance costs brought forward
- **property business profits** - the profits of the property business in the tax year (after using any brought forward losses)
- **adjusted total income** - the income (after losses and reliefs, and excluding savings and dividends income) that exceeds your personal allowance.

The tax reduction can't be used to create a tax refund. If the basic rate tax reduction is calculated using the 'property business profits' or 'adjusted total income' then the difference between that figure and 'finance costs' is carried forward to calculate the basic rate tax reduction in the following years.

Landlords who own their letting properties in a company are not affected by this and can claim the full amount of loan interest relief. However, the question of whether or not you can or should transfer your buy-to-let properties into a company is one which requires careful consideration and we recommend that you consult an accountant on this issue.

Joint tenants and tenants in common

While it may seem strange to refer to property owners as being tenants, those owning it as joint tenants own the property in equal shares. Those owning it as tenants in common own it in a nominated or chosen proportion which need not be equal.

One consequence of owning property as joint tenants is that on the death of one, his share passes automatically to the survivor. If the property is owned as tenants in common, on death the share doesn't pass automatically to the other owner.

Lease premiums and tax

Lease premiums are now becoming 'more a thing of the past', but if you do grant a lease of not more than 50 years' duration, for which you receive a premium, then you will be assessed for Income Tax on the premium. The taxable amount is quite complicated to calculate but (putting a block of ice on your head we will try to explain it): you take the premium and reduce it by 1/50 of its amount for each complete period of 12 months, other than the first 12 months, and this amount is subject to Income Tax. The balance of the premium is normally subject to Capital Gains Tax.

Leases and Stamp Duty

These are complicated so you should seek professional advice. In effect, if you take out a lease you are likely to have to pay Stamp Duty Land Tax (see page 149 for more information).

Annual Tax on Enveloped Dwellings (ATED)

In general terms, this is an annual tax charge which arises on a company which owns residential property in the UK, valued at more than £500,000. There are a number of exemptions from the charge, a common one being that the property is rented out. The table overleaf sets out the annual charges that are due.

An ATED return must be made within 30 days of the date on which the person first comes within the charge to ATED. A person who owns a single-dwelling interest on the first day of the chargeable period (1 April each year) will have a filing date for the return of 30 April. A return has to be submitted to HMRC even if full relief is available from the charge.

Property value	Annual charge 2021/22
£500,000 - £1,000,000	£3,700
£1,000,000 - £2,000,000	£7,500
£2,000,000 - £5,000,000	£25,300
£5,000,000 - £10,000,000	£59,100
£10,000,000 - £20,000,000	£118,600
More than £20,000,000	£237,400

CHAPTER 8

Income from dividends and interest

Tax payable on dividends received

If you receive more than £2,000 of dividends and your total income is within the basic rate band, i.e. not exceeding £52,270 in 2021/22, then tax is charged at 7.5 per cent on the dividends which exceed this tax-free allowance.

Do be aware, however, that the £2,000 tax-free allowance forms part of your basic rate band, therefore your income including the tax-free dividends must not exceed the sums just mentioned.

If you are a higher rate taxpayer (income between respective sums just mentioned and £150,000), then the dividends in excess of £2,000 are taxed at 32.5 per cent.

If you are an additional rate taxpayer (income in excess of £150,000) then your dividend income in excess of £2,000 is taxed at 38.1 per cent.

Tax payable on interest received

Most interest paid by banks, building societies and similar institutions is paid gross, i.e. they have not deducted any tax from it.

As well as bank and building society interest, the term 'interest' includes interest distributions from unit trusts, OEICs and investment trusts, income from government or company bonds, and most types of Purchased Life Annuity payments. Interest received on ISAs is not included as this is tax free.

Most people can earn some interest from their savings without paying tax.

Your allowance for earning tax-free interest is made up of the following:

- Personal Allowance
- Starting Rate for savings – depending on your other income
- Personal Savings Allowance – depending on your Income Tax band.

Personal Allowance

You can use your Personal Allowance (£12,570) to earn interest tax free if you haven't used it up on your wages, pension or other income.

Starting Rate for Savings

You can also get up to £5,000 of interest tax free. This is your starting rate for savings. The more you earn from other income (e.g. wages or pension), the less your starting rate for savings will be. If your other income is £17,570 or more, you're not eligible for the starting rate for savings. If your income is less than £17,570, your starting rate for savings is a maximum of £5,000. Every £1 of other income above your Personal Allowance reduces your starting rate for savings by £1.

Personal Savings Allowance

You may also get up to £1,000 of interest tax free, depending on which Income Tax band you're in.

This is your Personal Savings Allowance.

Income Tax band	Tax-free savings income
Basic rate	£1,000
Higher rate	£500
Additional rate	£0

Your allowance applies to interest from:

- bank and building society accounts
- savings and credit union accounts
- unit trusts, investment trusts and open-ended investment companies
- peer-to-peer lending
- government or company bonds
- life annuity payments
- some life insurance contracts

HMRC is likely to know what interest you have received

HMRC have access to tremendous amounts of data already, and this is increasing all the time. It is anticipated that HMRC will be informed of the amounts of bank and building society interest that you receive each year. Therefore, in theory, they should have the correct data for you. However, it is always prudent to check the figures that HMRC quote.

Tax payable on annuities

Annuities are sources of income usually enjoyed by the elderly. The individual makes an investment in the annuity and over the remaining period of his life receives payments in connection with this annuity, some of which is capital and some of which is taxable income. When the annuity is paid it will be clearly shown how much is capital (and this is not taxable), how much is income and how much tax has been deducted. You should total the income elements of each payment and enter the gross totals together with the tax deducted on your Tax Return.

ISAs

ISA stands for Individual Savings Account. They are free from Income and Capital Gains Tax.

There are four types:

1. **Cash and Stocks and Shares ISA.** You can put up to £20,000 in to one of these each year. You must be 16 or over for a Cash ISA and 18 or over for a Stocks and Shares ISA.

2. **Lifetime ISA.** This is designed to help you buy your first home or save for later life. You must be 18 or over but under 40 to open a Lifetime ISA. You can put in up to £4,000 each year, until you're 50. The government will add a 25 per cent bonus to your savings, up to a maximum of £1,000 per year. The Lifetime ISA limit of £4,000 counts towards your annual ISA limit of £20,000. You can hold cash or stocks and shares in your Lifetime ISA or have a combination of both. There's a 25 per cent charge to withdraw cash or assets from a Lifetime ISA; this doesn't apply if you're:

   • buying your first home;
   • aged 60 or over;
   • terminally ill, with less than 12 months to live.

3. **Junior ISA.** These are designed to help children save. Your child must be both under 18 and living in the UK. You can't have a Junior ISA as well as a Child Trust Fund – if you want to open a Junior ISA, ask a provider to transfer the Trust Fund into it. You can put in up to £9,000 each year.

4. **Innovative finance ISA.** An innovative finance ISA is a type of ISA that adds a tax-free wrapper to savings income from peer-to-peer lending, crowdfunding debentures and cash.

Venture Capital Trusts

Venture Capital Trusts were introduced to encourage individuals to invest indirectly in unquoted trading companies. If you do this, you will be exempt from Income Tax on dividends and Capital Gains Tax on sales of shares acquired of up to £200,000 a year. In addition, Income Tax relief of 30 per cent applies on up to £200,000 in any tax year, if you subscribe for new shares which you then hold for at least five years.

Enterprise Investment Scheme

The Enterprise Investment Scheme (EIS) was introduced to encourage individuals to invest directly in unquoted trading companies. If you make an EIS investment, you will be exempt from tax on capital gains (but not dividends) arising from shares acquired of up to £1 million a year. Also, if you subscribe for new shares which you then hold for at least three years, there is Income Tax relief based on 30 per cent of up to £1 million of that EIS investment in any tax year.

It's also possible to defer Capital Gains Tax on the gain arising on the sale of any asset by reducing that gain by the amount of EIS investment. The tax becomes payable when the EIS shares are sold.

There is an additional £1 million annual limit so long as at least £1 million is invested in 'knowledge intensive' companies.

Seed Enterprise Investment Scheme

The Seed Enterprise Investment Scheme (SEIS) is similar to the EIS, but it's aimed specifically at investments in small start-up businesses and has different rules. The company should be carrying on a qualifying trade, generally outside of finance or investment, have fewer than 25 employees, and have assets of less than £200,000. The subscriber can invest up to

£100,000 in a single tax year, with an overall maximum investment in each company of £150,000.

The investor must own less than 30 per cent of the business and it must be a UK company. The best bit is that 50 per cent tax relief is given on the investment regardless of the investor's marginal rate of tax. Like EIS investments, SEIS investments are free from Capital Gains Tax when sold, provided they have been held for at least three years. Any taxpayer who has a Capital Gains Tax liability will receive 50 per cent CGT relief when they reinvest those gains into SEIS companies.

REITs

A REIT is a Real Estate Investment Trust, a special type of investment trust designed to encourage investment in the property sector. It enables investors to invest in the property market without buying a property and provides tax breaks for property companies by exempting income and gains from tax.

Income paid to investors will be net of basic rate tax. So, if you receive a payment of £80, the gross figure you should put on your Tax Return is £100 from which tax at 20 per cent has been deducted and, if you are a basic rate taxpayer, no further tax is due. If you are liable to tax at 40 or 45 per cent, you will have to pay the extra 20 or 25 per cent under self-assessment. These payments are known as PIDs (Property Income Distributions). Just to make things confusing, some REITs will also pay dividends (see the first section of this chapter). The voucher that accompanies the payment should make it clear whether the payment is a PID or a dividend.

CHAPTER 9

Life assurance policies

The taxation of life assurance

There are three main types of life assurance:

- **Term Assurance.** The sum assured is only paid if you die during the term of the policy; there is no savings element in this policy, but they tend to be cheap.
- **Whole of life assurance**, whereby the sum is payable on your death at any time.
- **Endowment policy**, where the amount assured is payable on your death within the term of the policy or at the policy's end.

If you invest now in a life assurance policy (normally called 'Single Premium Bonds'), you will pay no basic rate Income Tax when you draw the money out from it. However, you may be liable to the balance between the higher rates of tax and the basic rate tax if certain circumstances apply.

If what follows sounds complicated, don't worry, because the life assurance company is bound to send not only you, but also HM Revenue & Customs (HMRC) a certificate detailing the information about your policy and the gain that you have made.

In principle, if you withdraw no more than five per cent of your investment each year, there will be no further tax implications on this sort of policy. If you withdraw more than five per cent, there may be tax to pay, but we do suggest that rather than going into complicated calculations, you should take advice from either HMRC or a qualified accountant.

Chargeable events

A chargeable event is when you withdraw money from a life assurance policy or bond. As you will see from the previous question, unless you withdraw more than five per cent of your investment in any tax year, there will be no tax implications. Indeed, even if you do withdraw more than five per cent, if you are a basic rate taxpayer, with the aid of top slicing relief there may not be any additional tax liability arising.

Bonds

There are all sorts of bonds, including Euro Bonds, Guaranteed Income Bonds and Single Premium Bonds. The subject of Euro Bonds doesn't fall into the scope of this book, but in the case of Guaranteed Income Bonds these resemble annuities and only the income element is subject to Income Tax.

In the case of chargeable income bonds, we refer you to the question above relating to the taxation of life assurance, where we hope you will find the answer.

Top slicing relief

Top slicing relief is complicated and we do suggest that, if you want a full answer which you will properly understand, you either call the HMRC Helpline 0300 200 3310 or refer to a professional adviser. Basically, it's a relief available to individuals (but not to companies) against what otherwise would be a higher rate of tax on any investment gain you might make on the surrender or sale of a life assurance policy.

Partial surrenders

If you make a partial surrender of a life assurance policy, and this is usually the case when you receive annual payments from a Single Premium Bond, it may give rise to tax but only if you withdraw more than five per cent of your original investment.

As with areas of this chapter on life assurance policies, we recommend you take professional advice, because the explanation of this complicated area of the tax law is beyond the ambit of this book.

Tax relief on permanent health insurance payments

Permanent health insurance policies are intended to provide you with an income should illness prevent you from working. If your employer pays the premium on your policy, it will obtain a tax allowance on the payment it makes and you will have to pay tax on any benefit that you receive.

If you make the payments yourself, whether as an employee or as a self-employed person, you won't obtain any tax relief, but any benefits paid to you under these circumstances will be tax free.

Purchased life annuities

Purchased life annuities are investments normally taken out by the elderly which receive favourable tax treatment but do contain substantial risk.

The basic principle is that you invest a lump sum with an insurance company; then each year, up until the day of your death, it will repay part of the capital together with interest. The interest is taxed but the capital is not. This is one way of increasing the spendable income of elderly people. However, the danger is that if an annuity is taken out on day one and the annuitant dies on day two, all the money is lost. You can guard against this possibility by obtaining a guarantee that income payments will be made for a minimum period of time, even if you die soon after purchasing the annuity. Since 2015 there is no maximum guarantee period although some providers go to a limit of 30 years. Typically, the most common guarantee periods are 5 to 10 years.

CHAPTER 10

Capital Gains Tax

Introduction to Capital Gains Tax (and a word of warning)

If you make a gain on the disposal of any investments, land and buildings, jewellery, antiques or any form of other property, you may be liable to Capital Gains Tax (CGT) on the gain. The main activities that we, as accountants, see our clients paying CGT on are the sale of businesses, stocks and shares, antiques worth over £6,000, property, and gifts of any of the above.

Here are some of the assets that are exempt from the CGT net:

- Private motor vehicles
- Your own home (but not including a second home)
- National Savings Certificates
- Foreign currency
- Decorations for gallantry (unless purchased)
- Betting winnings (including pools, lotteries and Premium Bonds)
- Compensation or damages for any wrong or injury suffered
- British government securities
- Life assurance policies and annuities
- Chattels (i.e. movable possessions) sold for £6,000 or less
- Assets given to a charity or the nation
- Enterprise and Seed Investment Scheme shares held for three years
- Timber and uncut trees
- Individual Savings Accounts
- Venture Capital Trust shares
- Guns, wine, antiques – providing they are not used in a business

- Debts
- Qualifying Corporate Bonds
- Child Trust Funds
- Cashbacks

The person making the gain is responsible for paying the CGT. However, where an asset is given away and the taxpayer may think that he has made no gain (because no money has been received) and therefore has no tax to pay, he may easily be mistaken. Because a gift constitutes a disposal, if there is a gain on that disposal, even the giver, who is in receipt of no disposal proceeds, pays CGT on the gain that he is deemed to have made on the disposal.

In general, to pay CGT one has to be a UK-resident taxpayer, which includes a company, trust or partnership. However, non-residents are now liable to capital gains made on the disposal of residential property. If you are resident but not domiciled in this country, you are only charged CGT on your overseas realisations of assets when you bring the money here.

A rough guide to Capital Gains Tax is provided at Appendix 7.

The taxation of Capital Gains

For individuals, the rate of CGT for non-property gains is 10 per cent for standard rate taxpayers and 20 per cent for higher rate taxpayers. This is charged on all gains above the annual exempt amount, which is £12,300 in the year ended 5th April 2022. The gain is treated as the top slice of income in order to determine whether it is chargeable wholly at 10 per cent or at a combination of 10 per cent up to the basic rate band limit and then 20 per cent on the remainder. The historical 18 per cent and 28 per cent rates continue to apply in a similar manner to disposals of residential property which do not qualify for Private Residence Relief and to disposals of carried interest. The chargeable gain is the difference between the sale proceeds (less costs of sale) and original cost or market value at 31 March 1982 if later, plus any improvement costs incurred in the intervening period. If the disposal was by way of gift, then you use market value as the disposal 'proceeds'. Capital losses may be deducted from capital gains or, if these are insufficient, carried forward to subsequent years.

The chargeable gains of companies are included in their total taxable profits for the relevant period. They are calculated as for individuals with two exceptions: firstly, companies may claim an Indexation Allowance to take account of inflation. The Retail Prices Index – from March 1982 onwards – is applied to the period of ownership of the asset to calculate this. But this allowance was frozen with effect from 1 January 2018. Secondly, a company does not have any annual exemption.

Business Asset Disposal Relief

Business Asset Disposal Relief, which was known as Entrepreneurs' Relief until 5 April 2020, gives preferential treatment to the disposal of business assets. This term includes a trading business carried on either alone or in partnership, assets of that business, shares in the individual's own trading company and assets owned by the individual but used in his trading company or business. Furnished holiday letting properties are also regarded as business assets, but not properties used for any other type of letting. Qualifying gains are taxed at a rate of 10 per cent.

There is a lifetime limit of £1 million upon which the Business Asset Disposal Relief can be claimed and claims can be made on more than one occasion to utilise the lifetime limit. The business must have been owned for at least two years ending on the date of the disposal. If you are selling a property that was used in the business, then you have to sell it within three years of selling the business or you will lose the relief on it.

Annual CGT exemption

Every year, there is an annual exemption from Capital Gains Tax. In 2021/22, your first £12,300 of gains is exempt. In the case of trusts, it's £6,150. The rate of Capital Gains Tax (CGT) is 20 per cent for trusts (28 per cent for disposals of residential property and carried interest).

Deductions that can be claimed in calculating a chargeable gain

You can set the costs of acquisition of the asset, including purchase price, and the sale costs, against the gain.

In addition, if you bought an asset on which you have incurred enhancement or improvement expenditure, then that too will be allowed as a cost. Certain costs such as accountant's fees are not allowed, but if you are looking for allowable costs, and because this subject can be so wide-ranging, we suggest you talk either to a professional accountant or to HM Revenue & Customs (HMRC).

Relief for capital losses

If you sell or give away a capital asset at a loss, it's normally deductible from any capital gains that you have made during the same year and any remaining unrelieved losses are available to carry forward against future capital gains. If you give or sell an asset to a 'connected person' (generally a blood relative or a business partner/fellow director), the loss can only be used against gains on assets given or sold to the same party.

However, there is some relief available from a different quarter. If you make a trading loss in your business and don't have enough income to cover it, you can elect for the unused losses from that trading period to be set against your capital gains for that same tax year or for the previous tax year. In other words, capital gains can be reduced by trading losses. Again, we would suggest that you seek professional advice on this.

There is also scope to claim Income Tax relief for capital losses arising on qualifying shares which have been subscribed for, against your general income either in the year of the loss or the previous tax year. Shares are qualifying shares if EIS relief is attributable to them, or where this is not the case, they are shares in a qualifying trading company which have been subscribed for by the individual.

The date for paying Capital Gains Tax

Capital Gains Tax is payable by individuals on 31 January following the end of the tax year in which the gain was made. It's payable by companies, along with the rest of their Corporation Tax, nine months after the year end.

However, if Capital Gains Tax is due on a sale or gift of a property, individuals only have 30 days from completion of the disposal to report to HMRC and pay the tax. You need to create a Capital Gains Tax on UK property account before you can report and pay the tax. If you're a resident or representing a trust, you can use this service to:

- report the disposal of UK residential property or land made from 6 April 2020;
- pay any tax you might owe for that disposal; and
- view and change your previous returns.

Part-disposals

Where part of an asset is disposed of, you have to work out the cost applicable to the part sold. The rules are complicated. A special rule applies to small part-disposals of land and, provided that the sale proceeds don't exceed either £20,000 or one fifth of the total market value of the land, you may deduct the sale proceeds from your base cost rather than pay any tax now.

Private residences and Capital Gains Tax

Normally, the house or flat in which you live is exempt from Capital Gains Tax when you sell it. The property must have been your only or main residence during the period of ownership. During the last nine months of ownership, the property is always regarded as your main residence even if you don't live there. Note that people who move into a care home or have a disability can claim for the last 36 months of ownership. You can also be absent for periods totalling three years and for any period throughout which you worked abroad. To qualify for these additional periods of exemption, you must live in the property both before and after the absence. In addition, if you had any work which required you to live in job-related accommodation, that also doesn't stand against you for Capital Gains Tax purposes. Any periods of absence in excess of the periods allowed result in the relevant proportion of your sale profit being charged to Capital Gains Tax.

You can also get relief for any period when your house was let up to a maximum of £40,000 (or the amount of Private Residence Relief whichever is the least per owner). Lettings relief is only available for people who were in shared occupancy with a tenant.

If a specific part of your house is set aside for business purposes, then that proportion of your profits on the sale of the house will be taxable. However, if you don't have any rooms used exclusively for business purposes you won't normally be liable to any Capital Gains Tax if you sell your house.

Special consideration needs to be given to houses with a lot of land alongside them. If land is sold in excess of what HMRC regards to be a normal area of garden in character for the house that is being sold, then the gain on the sale of such extra land will be subject to Capital Gains Tax.

Within two years of buying a second property, you should send in a letter (called an 'election') in which you disclose to the taxman which of your two properties you are treating as your private residence for Capital Gains Tax purposes. Otherwise, the taxman will decide for you and the decision will be based on the facts (i.e. where you have actually spent the majority of your time).

Chattels sold for less than £6,000

A chattel is an asset which is 'tangible movable property', such as a work of art or a set of chairs. Provided that the asset fetches no more than £6,000, HMRC doesn't require you to pay Capital Gains Tax on it. However, if you have a set of dining room chairs and each one is not worth £6,000 but in total the set is worth say £30,000, the set will attract Capital Gains Tax on it, because a set is treated as one chattel.

Relief for the sale of business assets

In principle, you are liable to Capital Gains Tax in respect of the sale of any assets used in your business. However, if all of the sale proceeds are invested in further business assets that are purchased within one year before or three years after the sale, you can claim Rollover Relief as a result of which the gain on the disposal is rolled over into the cost of the new business assets acquired. Therefore, no tax is paid until the new business assets are sold, unless they too are replaced. If a lesser amount is reinvested, a limited amount of Rollover Relief can still be available.

For these assets to qualify they must be either land and buildings, fixed plant and machinery, goodwill, milk and potato quota or other agricultural quotas including payment entitlements under the Single Payment Scheme. Please note that motor vehicles don't qualify.

Capital Gains Tax relief for gifts

In principle, gifts of assets don't escape Capital Gains Tax, but gifts of the following attract a special relief called Holdover Relief:

• Business assets
• Agricultural property
• Shares and securities in a family trading company
• A gift which gives rise to an immediate charge to Inheritance Tax

Holdover Relief works in the same way as Rollover Relief. The gain is held over until such time as the recipient of the gift sells it.

Gifts which attract Inheritance Tax are rare, but one such example is when you transfer assets into a discretionary trust. Gifts to individuals and to trusts for disabled people, are classed as potentially exempt transfers (PETs) and Inheritance Tax won't be payable, unless you die within seven years of making the gift. However, tapering relief may reduce the Inheritance Tax payable after three years.

CGT for those who live abroad

If you are resident in this country (see page 119 for further information on this term), you are liable to tax on any capital gains realised anywhere in the world. However, if you have realised a gain in a country which won't allow the proceeds to be sent to the UK, you can claim for the gain to be deferred until the year in which you receive the money in this country.

If you are non-resident in this country but are carrying on a trade in the UK, you are liable to CGT on the assets used in the business. If you are UK-domiciled, HMRC does have new powers to apportion certain capital gains of overseas trusts of which you are a beneficiary and this has caught out a number of wealthy people who transferred their assets abroad.

If you have left the UK for tax residence abroad, you will be liable to CGT on gains made when selling UK residential property. You will be liable on the gain which relates to the period after 5 April 2015. Therefore, you will either need to know the value of your property at 5 April 2015, or you can use a straight-line time apportionment over the entire period of ownership.

From 6 April 2019 the disposal of UK non-residential property is also caught by the legislation. Rebasing needs to be performed or calculated to 6th April 2019 when non-residential UK property is subsequently sold.

This is a complicated matter and professional advice should be sought. When obtaining property valuations, we would recommend at least two separate professional valuations, as this will reduce the risk of HMRC successfully arguing with your figures.

Generally speaking, if you are absent from the UK for at least five complete tax years, any other (non-residential) gains will be free from UK CGT.

Non-residents selling UK land or property must report the disposal to HMRC and pay any CGT due within 30 days of the sale.

Selling shares one day, to create enough gains to use up the annual Capital Gains Tax allowance, and buying them back the next day

If you sell shares and buy them back within 30 days (known as the 30-day rule), for CGT purposes the disposal of the shares is matched against the purchase cost of the shares acquired within 30 days of the sale, not against the original acquisition cost. However, you can get around this problem if your spouse buys the shares back on the open market, and not directly from you.

Deferment or avoidance of CGT

Providing certain conditions are met, if you invest disposal proceeds into an Enterprise Investment Scheme (EIS) which would otherwise be liable to CGT, the gain on your investment can be deferred. Providing all qualifying conditions are met, the gain on the disposal of the EIS investment can be free of any CGT liability.

It is also possible to make an investment into a Seed Enterprise Investment Scheme (SEIS) company of sale proceeds, subject to CGT. There is a maximum investment of £100,000 but the reinvestment of £100,000 would permit the gain chargeable to be reduced by £50,000. Any gain made on the SEIS investment will be free of CGT, providing the qualifying conditions are met.

So, there are ways of reducing chargeable gains, but we strongly recommend that professional financial advice be taken by anyone considering making EIS and SEIS investments. Risks and conditions are attached to these investments, which must be clearly understood in order to gain the best taxation outcome. Investments of this sort are not suitable for everyone.

CHAPTER 11

Trusts and estates

Introduction

A trust is brought into existence when a person (called the 'settlor') transfers some of his assets to trustees (who become the legal owners) for the benefit of third parties, called 'beneficiaries' (the beneficial owners). A trust is a legal entity in itself. Another word for a trust is a settlement. Sometimes trusts are created under a Will and sometimes they are created during the lifetime of the settlor. Sometimes trusts are created to save tax, sometimes to protect assets; there are many and various reasons for setting up a trust.

As far as the tax system is concerned, there are basically two types of trust: interest in possession trusts and discretionary trusts.

In the first type, one or more beneficiaries will have been given a life interest. This means that they are automatically entitled to the trust's income but have no right to the capital. The trust deed will specify who is the residual beneficiary who will get the capital and the income when the life tenant dies.

In the second type, there will be one or more beneficiaries who have no automatic right to either the capital or the income of the trust. The trustees will have discretion to decide to whom to pay any income or capital.

Trusts and Income Tax

Trustees have to complete a Trust and Estate Tax Return reporting their income and capital gains on an annual basis.

The trustees of interest in possession trusts pay tax at the appropriate basic rate of tax. The beneficiaries are then treated as having paid the tax that has been deducted by the trustees.

The trustees of discretionary trusts pay tax at the special rates of tax applicable to trusts. On trust income up to £1,000, dividend income suffers tax at 7.5%; all other income is taxed at 20%. On trust income over £1,000 dividend income suffers tax at 38.1% and all other income is taxed at 45%.

Certain trusts with vulnerable beneficiaries are able to elect that the trust income and gains are taxed at the beneficiaries' tax rate if this proves more beneficial.

The trustees must pay the tax on 31 January and 31 July each year.

Trusts in Wills

The main tax that affects Wills, triggered by the death of the testator, is Inheritance Tax and there is a separate section in this book dealing with this aspect. However, when someone dies his personal representative (PR) or executor will make sure that a personal Tax Return is completed from the start of the tax year to the date of the deceased's death. From the date of his death to the end of the tax year the PR will have to account for tax on the estate income and report to the beneficiaries on the tax that the PR has deducted. Each year the PR will have to submit a Trust and Estate Tax Return to HM Revenue & Customs (HMRC). However, in the year in which the estate is wound up and all the assets have been distributed, the PR will only have to account for the tax on the estate income up to the date of distribution. In practice, if probate value is less than £2.5 million and the total tax due by the PR is less than £10,000, HMRC will accept a single computation and one-off payment for the whole of the estate period.

Discretionary trusts and Inheritance Tax

The trustees of a discretionary trust don't pay Inheritance Tax on a death but instead pay Inheritance Tax on every tenth anniversary of the date of the settlement. The amount on which tax is charged is the total value of the chargeable assets in the trust less the nil rate band of £325,000. Most assets will have to be included but some may benefit from 100% Agricultural or Business Property Relief. The tax payable in respect of this periodic charge is 30 per cent of the lifetime rate, which is itself half of the rate on death. The rate of tax is therefore six per cent (i.e. 30 per cent of 20 per cent) of the chargeable assets in the trust, but the calculation is not an easy one and you should seek professional advice.

A discretionary trust also pays Inheritance Tax when any of the chargeable settled property leaves the trust. This is called an 'exit charge'. The rate of tax is determined by the length of time that has elapsed either since the creation of the trust or since the last periodic charge.

Trusts and Capital Gains Tax

Most trusts attract half the annual exemption that is available for individuals. This is currently half of £12,300, i.e. £6,150 (for 2021/22). The capital gains are worked out in accordance with the usual Capital Gains Tax rules (see chapter 10) and the tax on any capital gain is paid over at the same time as the balancing payment for the Income Tax, in other words 31 January following the end of the tax year. Trusts pay Capital Gains Tax at the rate of 20 per cent (or 28 per cent in the case of disposals of residential property or carried interest).

Setting up a trust

Gifts to either new or existing discretionary trusts are regarded as chargeable transfers for Inheritance Tax purposes. This means that transfers into them above the nil-rate band are likely to be subject to tax at 20 per cent.

For those who believe that distributing the assets in a trust to a beneficiary when they reach the age of 18 is too low, there is now a type of trust, known as an age 18 to 25 trust. A trust of this kind can only be set up under the Will of a deceased parent or under the Criminal Injuries Compensation Scheme. With such trusts, the beneficiary doesn't have to take capital at the age of 18 but must do so by the age of 25. For these trusts, there is no exit or ten-year charge while the beneficiary is under the age of 18. From 18 to 25 a reduced Inheritance Tax charge applies. The maximum payable is 4.2 per cent (instead of six per cent). Some parents may feel that paying tax at 4.2 per cent maximum is a better option than handing over a large capital sum to an 18-year-old.

Ending a trust

One should take legal advice before ending a trust but please be aware that not only are most trusts that were settled with a value above the nil rate band subject to the ten-year charge of six per cent, there is also an exit charge from such trusts.

When an interest in possession trust comes to an end but the property remains in trust, this is treated as the creation of new settled property. There is an immediate entry charge.

These charges do not apply to trusts for the disabled. Nor do they apply to a trust set up in a parent's Will for a minor child, so long as he is fully entitled to the assets at the age of 18.

The duties of trustees

As a firm we have acted for a number of trusts (both private and charitable) and are aware of a certain tendency towards general ignorance by some trustees of their responsibilities and duties. Accordingly, we thought it might be helpful if we set out what those duties and responsibilities are:

Trustees:

- Must always act in accordance with the terms of the trust deed as well as general law.
- Must ensure that all property owned by the trust is:
  - Held in the name of the trustees
  - Properly insured and
  - Used for the benefit of the beneficiaries of the trust.
- Must take professional advice on matters outside their personal skills.
- Must use any professional skills they have for the benefit of the trust. Hence professional trustees carry a higher level of responsibility than lay trustees.
- Should meet regularly – at least once a year.
- While they may delegate certain responsibilities to employees, they would still be responsible for the actions of those employees. In other words:
  - Where there is a management structure, those to whom management decisions have been delegated must both act within the terms of the responsibilities that have been delegated to them and report regularly to the trustees about their activities. In addition...
  - Where a trust borrows money, or where employees borrow money in the trust's name, this must be properly authorised.
- Must record their decisions, and any reasons behind their decisions, in case their decisions are challenged, possibly years later.
- Should excuse themselves from voting on any issue in which there might be a conflict of interest.
- Must not be seen to obtain any personal profit.

- Only professional trustees may charge for their services.

- If they are given discretion by the trust deed they must be aware of the terms of that discretion.

- Are obliged to invest, and manage, their investments under the Trustee Act 2000.

- Must inform beneficiaries, as well as HMRC, of the existence of the trust and must also report the trust's dealings appropriately to HMRC by means of Tax Returns, etc.

- Are obliged to prepare annual accounts and, in the case of large trusts, they should also prepare more frequent management accounts, including budgets and cash-flow forecasts etc.

- Are personally liable to make good, out of their own funds, any losses that a beneficiary might suffer as a result of any breach of duty they may exercise.

Trusts Registration Service

HMRC launched a Trusts Registration Service (TRS) in July 2017 for trustees to register their trust online.

Under existing self-assessment rules, the trustees (or their agents) must register details of a trust with HMRC by 5 October of the year after a liability to Income Tax or Capital Gains Tax (CGT) first arises. The registration process, which needs completing via TRS, includes providing information about the beneficial owners of the trust. In subsequent years, or where the trust is already registered for self-assessment, the trustees (or their agent) of either a UK or non-UK (express) trust that incur a UK tax liability are required to provide beneficial ownership information about the trust, using the TRS, by 31 January after the end of tax year.

This service provides a single online service for trusts to comply with their registration obligations, improve the processes around the administration of trusts, and allow HMRC to collect, hold and retrieve up-to-date information in a central electronic register.

CHAPTER 12

Corporation Tax

Introduction

Corporation Tax is the tax that limited companies and unincorporated associations (such as clubs) pay on their profits. It's a tax on the profits of the company; profits include trading profits, rental income, interest and capital gains.

The assessment and payment of Corporation Tax

A company accounts for Corporation Tax in 12-month periods, unless the accounting period from its starting to trade to the first accounting date, or the last period of trading , is less than 12 months. (You may already be thinking that it's time to consult a professional accountant and, in our view, if you have a limited company and you are dealing with Corporation Tax you should certainly seek professional advice.)

Every company has to fill in an annual Corporation Tax Return (Form CT600) and this Return has to be submitted by the company secretary or the directors within 12 months of the end of the accounting period. However, tax has to be paid, assuming we are dealing with a small company, just nine months after the end of the accounting period. Big companies have to pay Corporation Tax at more frequent intervals.

Corporation Tax self-assessment

Corporation Tax self-assessment means that companies have to work out their Corporation Tax liability themselves. Payment of the tax must be made electronically, which means either using online banking, or making payment at a bank or Post Office.

The submission of the Corporation Tax Return

All Corporation Tax Returns must be submitted to HMRC electronically along with the company accounts and Corporation Tax computations upon which they are based. Therefore, when the notice to complete a Corporation Tax Return arrives, we strongly suggest you send it to your accountant, if you have one.

The rate of Corporation Tax

The rate of Corporation Tax is 19 per cent. On 1 April 2023 this will rise to 25% for companies with profits over £250,000. The 19% rate will become a small profits rate payable by companies with profits of £50,000 or less. Companies with profits between £50,000 and £250,000 will pay tax at the main rate reduced by a marginal relief, providing a gradual increase in the effective corporation tax rate.

The definition of when a company starts to trade

A company is trading once it has sold something. It's also trading if it has been incorporated and has begun to develop and manufacture goods or services. Any loss that it makes will be carried forward until it makes its first profit. The loss can then be used to reduce the first profits.

Dormant companies and Corporation Tax

Dormant companies are, by definition, those that are doing nothing and, although a Corporation Tax Return may have to be submitted, there would be no profits and therefore no tax to pay. It's possible for a dormant company to do certain minor things (such as pay the annual return fee), but this doesn't include the earning of taxable profits.

Associated and subsidiary companies

Associated companies are those that are under common control or where one controls the other.

A subsidiary company is one that is either wholly or substantially owned by another company. A subsidiary company may surrender its losses to its holding company (or vice versa) thus allowing the holding company to set those losses off against its profits. This is called 'group relief'.

Close companies

A close company is, broadly speaking, a company that is under the control of five or fewer 'participators'. A participator is a person having a share or interest in the capital or income of the company. It's defined broadly to include, for example, any loan creditor of the company and any person who possesses a right to receive or participate in distributions of the company. A quoted company is not a close company if more than 35 per cent of its voting shares are owned by the general public.

When close companies make loans or distributions to their directors, tax is charged on the loan or distribution, unless the loan is repaid before the tax is due, i.e. nine months after the end of the company's financial year. If the loan is subsequently repaid, the company can get the tax back.

Public and private companies

A public company is a company:

- the Memorandum of Association of which states it to be a public company;
- that has been registered as such;
- whose name ends 'public limited company' or plc;
- which has an allotted share capital of not less than £50,000 of which at least 25 per cent has been paid on issue.

All other companies are private companies. A private company that incorporates some but not all of these features remains a private company.

Note: Although private companies have advantages over public companies, trading under any sort of incorporated structure attracts extra hassle and administration. Professional advice must be sought.

UK companies with overseas income

A company that has overseas income has to pay Corporation Tax on the gross amount of such income, but double tax relief is usually available. If a UK company receives a dividend from an overseas company from which tax has been deducted, the gross dividend is included in the taxable profits. However, there are other rules and we do suggest that you refer to specialist advice for help.

Companies that buy their own shares

In the case of a small company, it's frequently difficult for a buyer to be found for the shares of a shareholder who wishes to retire or sell up. There are rules which enable companies to buy their own shares but, once again, we suggest that professional advice is sought on this. Briefly, the rules are that:

- the company must not be quoted and should be trading, or be the holding company of a trading company;
- the purchase of the shares by the company must be mainly to benefit the trade of the company;
- the shareholder must be UK resident and must have owned the shares for at least five years. In addition, his shareholding must be substantially reduced, and this usually means by at least 25 per cent;
- if the payment is used to pay Inheritance Tax within two years after death, the above provisions do not apply.

To the extent that the amount paid for the shares exceeds the amount originally subscribed, there is deemed to be a distribution or dividend payable by the company to the shareholder concerned. This would normally be taxed as income in his or her hands. However, if advance clearance is obtained from HMRC, it is possible to get this payment taxed as a capital gain which will usually be advantageous to the shareholder.

The options for directors and/or shareholders taking payments from a company

In principle, you can either pay yourself a salary (which could be in the form of a bonus or other remuneration) or, so long as you hold shares in the company and there are the profits out of which to pay it, you could be paid a dividend.

If you are paid a salary, normal PAYE rules apply. If you are paid a dividend, the company doesn't have to pay any tax over at the time of making the distribution. This is because dividends can only be paid out of profits which have already been taxed. In principle, dividends are a more tax-efficient way of withdrawing profits from a company than salary. If you have lent money to your company and that company repays some or all of that loan , there is no tax involved with any such repayment.

Dividend payments by a company

The company accounts will show (one hopes) a profit. This profit figure will have deducted from it the amount of Corporation Tax that the company is due to pay on its profits. Whatever remains is added to the cumulative profits brought forward or deducted from the cumulative losses brought forward. A dividend can only be paid out of retained profits. If there are no retained profits – even though the company may have made a profit in its latest financial year – no dividend can be paid.

The company must be able to afford to pay a dividend to all of the holders of the class of shares on which the dividend is declared. This point is made because it is not possible for one shareholder to waive entitlement to a dividend and for another shareholder to therefore have a higher rate of dividend.

If there are undistributed profits brought forward, then these also can be distributed by way of a dividend.

If the company makes a loss, but there are greater undistributed profits brought forward than the loss, then a dividend can still be declared.

However, if the company makes a profit but there are greater losses than the profit brought forward, then a dividend cannot be declared because the profit must be used to reduce the accumulated losses.

Loss relief

This is a large subject, but we will try to give the basic rules as simply as we can.

A trading loss made in an accounting period can be set off against any other income and gains of the same period. Any remaining loss can then be carried back against the trading profits for the preceding year or it can be carried forward and set off against the trading profits of future years. A trading loss in the final period can be carried back for three years.

Extended Loss Carry Back

This temporary relief is available to both companies and unincorporated businesses. For accounting periods ending between 1 April 2020 and 31 March 2022, trading losses can be carried back three years, with losses required to be set against profits of most recent years first before carry back to earlier years.

The amount of loss that can be carried back to the earlier two years of the extended period is capped for each of those two years. This is a cap of £2,000,000 of losses for all relevant accounting periods ending in the period 1 April 2020 to 31 March 2021 (financial year 2020). A separate cap of £2,000,000 applies for all relevant accounting periods ending in the period 1 April 2021 to 31 March 2022 (financial year 2021). Groups are subject to a group cap of £2,000,000 for each relevant period.

Extended loss carry back claims are required to be made in a return. However, claims below a de minimis limit of £200,000 may be made outside a return. This means that any stand-alone or group company with losses capable of providing relief up to a maximum of £200,000 may make a claim in respect of a relevant accounting period without having to wait to submit its company Tax Return.

Any stand-alone company or group company wishing to make a claim exceeding £200,000 is required to make the claim in their company Tax Return.

Group relief

The trading losses of members of a group of companies can be used to reduce the trading profits of other members of the group, provided that:

- a claim is made within two years of the end of the accounting period;
- the companies participating in the group relief claim are all based in the UK and the parent has at least 75 per cent interest in each of the subsidiaries, directly or indirectly. A company may be based outside of the UK without jeopardising the existence of a group but it may not itself participate in the relief.

Please note that even though the parent may only own 75 per cent of the shares, it's entitled to 100 per cent of the relief. Also note that capital losses cannot be group relieved.

There are complicated rules where a company joins or leaves a group during an accounting period – this is another reason for seeking professional advice.

Companies and capital gains

Companies pay Corporation Tax on their capital gains. Companies can claim indexation relief (unlike individuals, partnerships and trusts) but this relief has been frozen with effect from 1 January 2018. This means that no relief is available for inflation accruing after this date.

Trading losses in accounting periods may be set off against not only gains, but also trading profits of the same period or indeed the previous period. Capital losses incurred by a company can only be offset against capital gains of the company in the same period or future accounting periods.

The Rollover Relief, which is described in the Capital Gain Tax chapter, is also available to companies. In addition, if one company in a group has a gain, another company in the group can purchase a qualifying business asset and roll the gain into the purchase, deferring any charge to Corporation Tax. Similarly, if one company has unused capital losses and another group company is to make a disposal which results in a capital gain, the company with the losses can be deemed to be making the disposal so that its losses can be used against the gain.

The rules are complicated and professional advice must be sought.

A director who borrows money from his or her company

In principle, it's unlawful for a director to borrow money from his own company. Small expense sums are allowed to be borrowed in advance. If the loan has not been repaid nine months after the end of the company's financial year, tax at the rate of 32.5 per cent has to be paid on the sum borrowed (this sum is repaid by HMRC when the loan is repaid and it would be reported on the next CT600 submitted after repayment). If no interest or a beneficial rate of interest is paid on the loan (unless the loan is for £10,000 or less), a benefit in kind arises on which the director must pay Income Tax and the company must pay Class 1A National Insurance contributions.

Companies and capital allowances

The normal capital allowances and annual investment allowance rules for businesses apply to companies, but there are special rules and we suggest that professional advice is sought.

Super-deduction

Between 1 April 2021 and 31 March 2023, companies investing in qualifying new plant and machinery will benefit from new first year capital allowances.

Under this measure a company will be allowed to claim:

- A super-deduction, providing allowances of 130% on most new plant and machinery investments that ordinarily qualify for 18% main rate writing down allowances.
- A first year allowance of 50% on most new plant and machinery investments that ordinarily qualify for 6% special rate writing down allowances.

This relief is not available for unincorporated businesses.

In a 'mixed partnership', where one of the partners is a company or a trust, you cannot use the annual investment allowance, only capital allowances.

Capital Allowance rates for different assets, from 1 April 2021:

	Super-deduction (130%)	50% FYA	100% FYA	AIA (100% on 31/12/21)	18% WDA	6% WDA
New 'main rate'[1] assets	✔			✔	✔	
Used assets				✔	✔	✔
Assets held for leasing				✔	✔	✔
New Integral Features[2]		✔		✔		✔
New long-life assets[3]		✔		✔		✔
New electric cars (0% emissions)			✔			
New cars with emissions 1-50g/km					✔	
All other cars						✔

[1] **Main rate** refers to the pool of plant and machinery.

[2] **Integral features** are lifts, escalators, moving walkways, space and water heating systems, air conditioning and air cooling systems, hot and cold water systems, electrical and lighting systems and external solar shading.

[3] **Long-life assets** are assets with a useful life of at least 25 years but put them in a main rate pool if their total value is less than £100,000.

Personal Service Companies and IR35

The so-called IR35 rules prevent someone (a worker) who works predominantly for just one business (a client) trading as a limited company (the intermediary) and then paying himself dividends from the profits, thus avoiding National Insurance altogether.

Before we outline the rules, here are some definitions:

A worker will be caught by the rules if he:

- trades as a limited company (the intermediary); and
- controls more than five per cent of the dividends; and
- receives or could receive payments from the intermediary which under

normal circumstances would be paid to him as salary.

Partnerships are also caught if:

- the worker, together with his close family, is entitled to more than 60 per cent of the profits of the partnership; or
- most of the profits come from working for a single client; or
- a partner's profit share is based on his income from relevant contracts.

Now for the rules:

In the circumstances where a worker provides his services to one client for a contract lasting for more than a month, the rules state the following:

- You take the amount of cash and non-cash benefits received by the intermediary.
- You then deduct any salary (actual salary) paid by the intermediary to the worker.
- You also deduct an allowable expense claim, which is a flat rate allowance of a total of:
  - the business mileage allowances for travel to each engagement;
  - five per cent of the expenses paid by the intermediary for the contracts;
- the expenses normally allowed to an employee;
  - the capital allowances normally allowed to an employee; • the employer's pension contributions;
  - the employer's National Insurance contributions.
- The balance (called 'deemed salary') is then treated as pay. Tax and National Insurance have to be applied accordingly.
- The tax and National Insurance arising on the balance are payable by 22 April after the year with interest running on late payments.
- Unpaid amounts can be recovered from the worker if the intermediary doesn't pay up.

There is one final twist: the deemed salary is not regarded as wages for the purpose of the National Minimum Wage, so the actual salary must be sufficient to meet the minimum wage requirements.

This is a nightmare, although it should be said that all other employees who are taxed under PAYE are following the proper rules, so why not these workers as well?

There are ways to escape from this net, but space is not available here to explain what needs to be done. However, even if it's possible to escape, certain clients insist that their workers do trade as a limited company, to save themselves having to apply PAYE.

The Corporation Tax treatment of research and development expenditure (R&D)

This is a very specialised area and there are a number of providers of advice and guidance in this field. The expertise mainly relates to what expenditure qualifies as R&D and how direct and overhead costs, e.g. staff wages, are attributed to particular innovative projects. If your company is spending money on R&D the tax breaks are really quite generous. It can claim 230 per cent of its qualifying costs against its profits or, if it is loss making, it can claim a tax credit worth up to 14.5% of the surrenderable loss.

To claim the relief you need to be a small or medium sized enterprise (SME) and show how your project meets the HMRC definition of R&D.

Companies who are making their first R&D claim can qualify for Advance Assurance. If Advance Assurance is granted, any R&D claims in the first three accounting periods will be accepted if they're in line with what was discussed and agreed. You can claim R&D tax relief if you're a SME with less than 500 staff and a turnover of under €100m or a balance sheet total under €86m.

Large companies can claim a Research and Development Expenditure Credit (RDEC) for working on R&D projects.

CHAPTER 13

Non-residence and working overseas

Tax domicile

Your domicile is the country which you regard as your natural home and the place where you intend to return in the event of going abroad. For most people it's the country of their birth and, unlike tax residence, it's not possible to have two domiciles under English law.

The arising basis provides that you are taxed on your income as it arises and wherever it arises. The remittance basis, on the other hand, provides what may be viewed as a 'deferral' of the UK tax charge in respect of foreign income and gains, that is, there is no charge when these foreign income or gains arise or accrue. Instead, foreign income and gains are only taxed in the UK when they are 'remitted' to the UK. If foreign income and gains remain offshore and are never regarded as remitted to the UK, the tax charge is effectively deferred indefinitely.

You are taxed on the arising basis on your worldwide income and gains if you:

- were born in the UK and have a UK domicile of origin and
- were resident in the UK for at least 15 of the 20 tax years immediately before the relevant tax year.

If you are non-domiciled but have been resident in the UK for more than seven of the past nine years and you want to claim the remittance basis of assessment, you will have to pay an annual charge of £30,000 on top of the UK tax on your overseas income and gains that you bring to the UK. The figure is £60,000 if you been UK resident for 12 of the past 14 years. These charges do not apply if the unremitted income or gains are less than £2,000 and, if this is the case, UK personal allowances and the annual capital gains allowance are also available.

This is a complex area and anyone affected should seek specialist advice.

Statutory Residence Test

The Statutory Residence Test is designed to provide greater certainty as to whether or not individuals are UK resident for tax purposes. This test does not have retrospective effect but it could be the case that somebody who was previously non-UK-resident becomes UK-resident following the application of this test.

There are a number of stages to the test and a variety of rules to apply to determine an individual's status. It is split into a number of components:

- Automatic Overseas Tests
- Automatic Residence Tests
- Sufficient Ties Test

The basic rules are that you are non-UK-resident in a tax year if you meet any of the Automatic Overseas Tests. But you are UK-resident if you do not meet any of the Automatic Overseas Tests and you meet one of the Automatic Residence Tests, or the Sufficient Ties Test.

Automatic Overseas Tests

If you meet any one of these tests, you are non-UK-resident:

1. You were resident in the UK for one or more of the previous three tax years and you spend fewer than 16 days in the UK in the tax year.

2. You were not resident in the UK for any of the three preceding tax years and you spend fewer than 46 days in the UK in the tax year.

3. You work full-time overseas throughout the tax year without any significant breaks, and:
   a) you spend fewer than 91 days in the UK in the tax year;
   b) the number of days in the tax year on which you work for more than three hours in the UK is less than 31.

If, having taken this test, you are not conclusively non-resident, then you must move on to the Automatic Residence Test.

Automatic Residence Tests

If you meet any one of these tests, you will be automatically UK-resident:

1. You spend 183 days or more in the UK in the tax year.

2. You have a home in the UK during all or part of the tax year. You will meet this test if there is at least one period of 91 consecutive days, at least 30 of which fall into the tax year, when you have a home in the UK in which you spend a sufficient amount of time and you either:

a) have no overseas home; or

b) have an overseas home or homes in each of which you spend no more than a permitted amount of time.

If you have more than one home in the UK, you should consider each of those homes separately to see if you meet the test. You need only meet this test in relation to one of your UK homes.

3. You work full-time in the UK for any period of 365 days, with no significant break from UK work, and:

a) all, or part, of that 365-day period falls within the tax year;

b) more than 75 per cent of the total number of days in the 365-day period when you do more than three hours of work are days when you do more than three hours work in the UK;

c) at least one day which is both in the 365-day period and in the tax year is a day on which you do more than three hours of work in the UK.

Sufficient Ties Test

If you do not meet any of the Automatic Overseas Tests or any of the Automatic Residence Tests, you should use the Sufficient Ties Test to determine your UK residence status for a tax year. You will need to consider your connections to the UK, called ties, and determine whether your ties, taken together with the number of days you spend in the UK, are sufficient for you to be considered UK-resident for tax purposes for a particular tax year.

If you were not UK-resident for any of the three tax years before the tax year under consideration, you will need to consider if you have any of these UK ties:

1. Family: spouse, civil partner, partner, or minor children, in the UK.

2. Accommodation: having accommodation in the UK which is available for a continuous period of at least 91 days and you spend at least one night there.

3. Substantive work in the UK: 40 working days or more (a working day is defined as more than three hours of work).

4. UK presence in the previous two tax years: more than 90 days in either of the previous two tax years.

5. More days spent in the UK in a tax year than in any other single country: this applies to leavers only and is designed to catch leavers who do not take up residence in any other country following a period of UK residence.

The number of days you spend in the UK in a tax year will dictate the number of UK ties that are needed for you to be UK resident.

Days in UK	Arrivers – not resident in the UK in the previous three years	Leavers – resident in the UK in at least one of the previous three tax years
Less than 16	Always non resident	Always non resident
16 – 45 days	Always non resident	Resident only if at least four ties apply
46 – 90 days	Resident only if at least four ties apply	Resident only if at least three ties apply
91 – 120 days	Resident only if at least three ties apply	Resident only if at least two ties apply
121 – 182 days	Resident only if at least two ties apply	Resident only if at least one tie applies
183 days or more	Always resident	Always resident

Residence and the taxation of income

If you are resident in this country, all normal taxable income, whether arising here or overseas, is taxable. However, if you are non-resident and you receive income from self-employment, partnerships or employment, all of which are carried out abroad, it will be tax free in this country. In fact, if you are non-resident, then the only income that is taxable in the UK is income arising in the UK, e.g. property income. The rules are complicated so any aspect that needs further consideration should be referred for professional advice.

Double taxation relief

The UK government has entered into Double Tax Agreements with many overseas countries (more than 130), the purpose of which is to prevent income and capital gains being taxed in both countries. So, where income or capital gains have already been taxed in another country, in principle the foreign tax counts towards your UK tax bill. However, such overseas tax is not refundable if it exceeds the UK tax due. Do be aware that, in some cases, not all the foreign tax can be set against your UK tax. If this happens, then you have to reclaim the balance from the overseas country – and that can be a nightmare!

Going abroad and becoming a non-UK tax resident

In principle, someone going to work full-time abroad under a contract of employment will be treated as non-resident from the date he leaves the UK. He must stay overseas for at least a full tax year. Visits to the UK are allowed but must be less than the permitted limit as specified in the calculation for split-year treatment. If you go abroad for any other reason, HMRC may give a temporary non-residence ruling and then review the position after three full years.

Tax payable on foreign income

If you are a UK resident, you pay normal UK tax on income from abroad, but if any of that foreign income has already suffered Income Tax in the country of origin, then it's more than likely that double taxation relief will result in that tax going towards paying your UK tax bill. However, the foreign tax cannot be refunded if it exceeds your UK tax liability. (You may find that Appendix 12 is helpful.)

Tax payable on professions conducted partly abroad

If you work in any profession that is conducted partly within this country and partly overseas, you will normally be assessed to UK tax on your entire profits and it's only if you conduct a separate profession entirely abroad that special rules will apply.

Tax payable on earnings from overseas employment

Again, this is a tricky area. If you go to work abroad part way through a tax year, you may qualify for split-year treatment. There are a number of circumstances where you might meet the criteria for split-year treatment, so we would advise you to seek professional help if you believe that this could apply to you.

Non-UK residents and tax allowances

You may be able to claim UK tax allowances if you are not resident here. If you are eligible to claim, you will generally be given the same allowances (i.e. the personal allowance) as an individual resident here. The following can claim, as well as certain others:

- A resident of the Isle of Man or the Channel Isles
- A citizen of the Commonwealth
- A citizen of a state within the European Economic Area
- A present or former employee of the British Crown

Letting out one's home while resident abroad

You will be liable to UK tax on the net rental income (i.e. gross rents less allowable expenses). Strictly speaking, the letting agent, or the tenant if there is no letting agent, should deduct tax at basic rate before paying the rent to you. However, you can apply to HMRC for a certificate authorising rental payments to be paid without deduction of tax.

You will still be entitled to your personal allowance and it may be that some of the tax that is deducted can be refunded to you. We strongly suggest you employ the services of an accountant to look after this for you.

Avoiding Capital Gains Tax by being resident abroad

This is a complicated matter and professional advice should be sought. If you are a non-UK resident, you will be liable to Capital Gains Tax on gains made on the disposal of residential property in the UK. (See chapter 10, on Capital Gains Tax.) For any other gains, on the disposal of shares for example, there is no CGT liability if you have been non-resident for at least five complete tax years.

Tax responsibilities for those who have just arrived in the UK to take up work here

In principle, you should contact the authorities or your employer will do this for you and from that day, even if it's the last day of the tax year, you will be entitled to the normal personal allowances. Equally, from that day you will be subject to Income Tax and National Insurance because you will be treated as a UK tax resident.

If you are self-employed or have income arising from a partnership or self-employment abroad or indeed interest arising abroad, then if you are UK resident but not UK domiciled, you will pay tax on income brought to the UK. If you are UK resident and UK domiciled, you will pay UK tax and may be able to claim double tax relief.

What overseas income will be subject to tax for those who have just arrived in the UK

It depends on your residence and domicile status. See the final paragraph in the section above.

CHAPTER 14

Inheritance Tax

Note: All references to married couples include same-sex couples who have registered as civil partners.

Introduction to Inheritance Tax

Inheritance Tax is a tax on the transfer of wealth in certain defined circumstances. Succeeding Estate Duty and then Capital Transfer Tax, it was introduced in the 1986 Finance Act and, although it's a highly complicated tax, certain basic information is included in this book.

Inheritance Tax covers transfers of value on death and also chargeable lifetime transfers, such as transfers to discretionary trusts (unless they are set up for a disabled person). Chargeable transfers on death are taxed at nil on the first £325,000 and 40 per cent thereafter. Chargeable lifetime transfers are taxed at nil on the first £325,000 and 20 per cent thereafter. They may also be charged again on death if this occurs within seven years of the transfer, but credit will be given for any lifetime tax paid.

Transfers to individuals and non-discretionary trusts are called 'potentially exempt transfers' or PETs. No Inheritance Tax is payable on these but, if they occur within seven years of the transferor's death, they are added to the value of his estate on death.

It's worth bearing in mind that, starting at 40 per cent, Inheritance Tax is reaping far more for the Treasury than it used to and so it's a tax which should be attended to and, where possible, planning to minimise it should be put in place.

The estates of armed forces personnel, emergency services personnel and humanitarian aid workers who died on or after 19 March 2014 and whose death was caused or hastened by injury while on active service, are exempt from Inheritance Tax.

Paying Inheritance Tax

Inheritance Tax in respect of chargeable transfers on death is due six months from the end of the month of the death. If a chargeable lifetime transfer is made between 6 April and 30 September, the due date is 30 April in the following year. If the chargeable lifetime transfer is made between 1 October and 5 April, the due date is six months after the end of the month in which the transfer is made.

What to consider when approaching the subject of Inheritance Tax

As practising accountants, we hardly ever deal with Inheritance Tax matters ourselves, but we have been able to observe the way in which it's dealt with by other professional advisers.

Our view is that if you are worried about Inheritance Tax, you should not go to a solicitor for advice but rather to a specialist Inheritance Tax adviser. While we don't like commenting on other professionals, we think that the following analysis is fair and appropriate. Chartered Accountants in practice are extremely competent at Income Tax, Capital Gains Tax, Value Added Tax as well as other accounting functions, but on the whole we should not advise our clients on matters of law. When it comes to solicitors, while they are very competent at matters of law, in our opinion only those who have the appropriate training and experience should advise their clients on matters of tax and particularly Inheritance Tax, where we have seen a number of bad mistakes made by people who have not been properly trained, who 'didn't know what they were doing'. So, our advice is that Inheritance Tax planning should be dealt with by a specialist in Inheritance Tax matters. This is how we run our practice and how we advise our clients whenever they need Inheritance Tax advice.

Making a Will

We always ask our clients if they have made a Will and try to make sure that, if they haven't, they do so quickly. If you haven't made a Will, the chances are that, when you die, your assets won't go to the people you would like them to go to. It's not expensive drawing up a Will and we would strongly suggest you go to a solicitor to do so. However, in view of our comments about Inheritance Tax planning, we think it would be a good idea for you to ensure, before you visit the solicitor, that you have listed your assets, applied a rough valuation to them and seen if the

Inheritance Tax bill for your estate is one that you are prepared to pay. If you are frightened by the size of the Inheritance Tax bill, then we suggest that you go to an Inheritance Tax specialist. Then, when you go to your solicitor, you can be armed with not only what you want to happen but also how you want the Inheritance Tax matters to be dealt with. If you don't do it this way round, you may find that you have a solicitor who thinks he knows about Inheritance Tax making all the plans for you and in our experience this can often end in problems. However, you do need to make a Will.

A template to help you work out your Inheritance Tax bill and plan to make a Will is provided at Appendix 8.

Choosing executors

In our view, it's extremely important to appoint executors whom your survivors like. We have seen cases where the executors who have been appointed were not liked by the surviving spouse and the misery caused by the death of the testator was exacerbated by the insensitivity of the executors. Therefore, don't choose your own friends just because you like them. Make sure your spouse likes them too and is happy for them to be appointed.

The nil-rate band rules

The nil-rate band is £325,000. Married couples and civil partners inherit each other's unused element of the nil-rate band on first death. So, couples have a joint nil-rate band of £650,000. If the couple's joint estate falls within the joint nil-rate band, they no longer have to worry about Inheritance Tax.

For everyone else, including unmarried couples, siblings living together and carers who have lived in and inherited the family home, the nil-rate band is £325,000 each, but they have no joint band.

The residence nil-rate band

There is an additional nil-rate band of £175,000 when a residence is passed on death to a direct descendant. Any unused residence nil-rate band can be transferred to a surviving spouse or civil partner.

The additional nil-rate band is also available when a person downsizes or ceases to own a home and assets of an equivalent value, up to the value of the additional nil-rate band, are passed on death to direct descendants.

There is a tapered withdrawal of the additional nil-rate band for estates with a net value of more than £2 million. This is at a withdrawal rate of £1 for every £2 over this threshold.

The effect of this is that it is possible for a property worth £1 million to be passed on by a married couple to their children free of Inheritance Tax, assuming they have no other assets.

General principles to remember, and the golden rules to apply when planning to reduce Inheritance Tax

This is such a big subject and the sums involved are so potentially enormous that we would not presume to give anything more than general advice in a book of this nature. However, there are certain general principles which we believe to be sound:

- Don't give everything away before you die; if you do and you keep on living, what will you live on?
- Consider taking advice from an Inheritance Tax specialist.
- Keep your Will up to date.
- Let your survivors know in advance if their lives are likely to be radically affected by your death. There is this problem that Wills generate great anticipation and anxiety and it's as well not to be too secretive about what you are proposing to do, so as to reduce extra stress and burdens on your survivors after you have died.

The Golden rules

1. **List your assets and decide to whom you would like them to pass.**

   Why not use the sheet in Appendix 8

2. **Make a Will.**

   If you don't make a Will, the chances are that your assets on your death won't be distributed according to your wishes. However, before you make a Will, it would be a good idea to attend to item 1 so that when you visit your solicitor you can 'hit the ground running' and, at the outset, tell him what you want your Will to say.

3. **Calculate the Inheritance Tax due.**

   Again, use Appendix 8 for this purpose.

4. **Decide how seriously you view the impact of any Inheritance Tax payable.**

   If you can tolerate the impact that Inheritance Tax may make on both your estate and your successors, then, so long as you have made a Will, you can probably rest at ease. However, having said 'probably', do remember that Inheritance Tax at 40 per cent can make a serious dent in your estate and, assuming you are not a tax expert, you might possibly overlook something and the situation may not be as favourable as you suppose. Accordingly, you may be well advised to take professional advice and get your Inheritance Tax calculation checked. As we say elsewhere in this chapter, the best professional advice on Inheritance Tax mitigation is to be gained from someone who specialises in Inheritance Tax mitigation and not necessarily from a high street accountant, financial adviser or solicitor. Therefore, choose your Inheritance Tax adviser very carefully.

5. **If you have an Inheritance Tax problem, then consult a suitably qualified adviser on how to mitigate the charge.**

   Then, having received such expert advice, set about putting his recommendations in place.

6. **If you want to take some elementary steps to reduce the impact of Inheritance Tax, and if you do nothing else, please at least consider the following possible courses of action:**

   - If you are currently unmarried or not in a civil partnership and you are facing an Inheritance Tax bill on your death, then we strongly suggest you follow steps 1 to 4 above.
   - If you survive your spouse or civil partner, bear in mind that your executors will be able to utilise their unused nil-rate band.
   - Married couples and civil partners should review the ownership of the property they occupy.
   - When it comes to passing investments to your children, there are a number of excellent financial products (such as loan trusts and discounted gift schemes) which we have seen used to very good effect. One of the beauties of these schemes is that, while ensuring that the capital passes to the next generation in a tax efficient way, they can also (and usually do) increase your annual spending money.
   - If you can afford to do so, use the nil-rate band to good effect. If you were to give away 1/7 of the nil-rate band every year (£46,428), by the time year seven had arrived, and assuming you are still alive, you would have given away at least £325,000 tax free. In year eight, the

first gift would drop out of the equation, in year nine, the second, and so on. If both you and your spouse do this, then you can give away £92,856 per year. However, do take professional advice.

- If you invest in shares in unquoted trading companies (including some shares listed on the Alternative Investment Market), once you have owned them for two years, they should qualify for 100 per cent Inheritance Tax Business Property Relief. However, be careful as the value of shares can just as easily go down as up.

- As part of your Inheritance Tax planning, try to ensure that you will have enough left after making any gifts to live on.

Beware of periodic charges

Discretionary trusts are subject to a charge to Inheritance Tax every ten years. In many cases, the trust is able to take advantage of the nil-rate band (£325,000 for 2021/22) and so no tax is payable. Any value in excess of this is charged at 30 per cent of the lifetime rate of 20 per cent, i.e. six per cent.

Quick succession relief

If, after someone dies and Inheritance Tax is paid on his estate, a beneficiary dies within five years, quick succession relief may be available and the tax payable on the second death thereby reduced. That said this relief is often of little value because of the way that the IHT rules work.

Inheritance Tax loss relief

The executors can submit an inheritance tax loss relief claim if they sell qualifying securities within 12 months of the date of death if the gross sale value is less than the probate value.

The claim needs to be submitted within four years from the end of the period in which the claim could arise, i.e. within five years in total from the date of death.

Qualifying investments are:

- Shares and securities listed on a recognised stock exchange at the date of death
- UK government stock
- Holdings in unit trusts and open-ended investment companies

The same principle applies for properties and land. Executors have four years from the date of death to sell a property asset. If the asset sells for less than the probate value, the executors can submit an IHT loss relief claim for the difference.

The claim needs to be submitted within three years from the end of the period in which the claim could arise, i.e. within seven years in total from the date of death.

CHAPTER 15

VAT

Introduction to VAT

Value Added Tax is a tax imposed when goods or services are sold. Any business which has a turnover in excess of £85,000 in the year beginning 1 April 2021 should – unless the business makes exclusively exempt supplies – register for VAT and add VAT to its VAT-able supplies. This threshold applies to a rolling 12 months' turnover, regardless of the accounting date of the business.

This is a complicated subject and anyone running a business with a turnover approaching £85,000 should seriously consider contacting an accountant to discuss whether he should register for Value Added Tax with HMRC.

In the case of businesses with a turnover in excess of £85,000, they certainly should take professional advice because they may be starting to get into deep trouble.

Making Tax Digital (MTD) for VAT

If you run a VAT-registered business with a taxable turnover above the VAT registration threshold (currently £85,000) you are required to keep digital VAT business records and send returns using MTD-compatible software.

Since MTD will shortly affect Income Tax as well as VAT, we have started a new chapter, number 19, that deals with this important development. Please refer to that chapter for more information on MTD for VAT.

Exempt supplies

Exempt supplies are outside the scope of VAT. If you only make exempt supplies, yours is an exempt business and you cannot register for VAT and you cannot recover any VAT on costs attributable to making the exempt supplies.

The following are exempt supplies:

- Land (this includes the sale of land and buildings, leases and rents)
- Insurance
- Postal services
- Betting, gaming and lotteries
- Finance
- Education
- Health and welfare
- Burial and cremation
- Subscriptions to trade unions, professional and other public interest bodies
- Sport, sports competitions and physical education
- Works of art – certain disposals exempted from capital taxes
- Fund-raising events by charities and other qualifying bodies
- Cultural services – admission to museums, exhibitions, zoos and performances of a cultural nature supplied by public bodies and eligible bodies
- Supplies of goods where input tax cannot be recovered
- Investment gold
- Cost sharing

Partial exemption

If you are VAT-registered because you sell a mixture of taxable and exempt goods and/or services and you incur VAT on any items that will be used to make exempt supplies, you are classed as partly exempt. As a general rule, you will not be able to reclaim exempt input tax. However, provided the amount of exempt input tax is below a certain amount, it can be recovered in full.

When you prepare your VAT Return, you claim the VAT directly attributable to your taxable supplies and you ignore completely the VAT directly attributable to your exempt supplies. When it comes to any input VAT that is attributable to both your taxable and your exempt supplies (your residual input tax), you have to use a partial exemption calculation to work out how much you can claim. You can use either HMRC's standard method or a tailor-made method which you have agreed with HMRC.

If the sums involved are small, there is a de minimis exemption which allows you to claim all your input tax notwithstanding the fact that some of it is attributable to exempt supplies. You can claim all the input tax you have incurred in any tax period if the total value of your exempt input tax is not more than:

- £625 per month on average;
- half of your total input tax in the relevant period.

Accounting records that must be kept by a VAT-registered business

With the introduction of Making Tax Digital for VAT (MTD) from 1 April 2019 all compulsorily VAT registered businesses need to keep their records electronically. However, if you are VAT registered, but your turnover is below the VAT registration limit we strongly suggest that you keep records, either on a computer or in a cash analysis book.

In addition to this, you need to keep your invoices on which you have claimed back VAT input tax. You also need to keep copies of your sales invoices on which you have recorded your output tax; all of your VAT records should be kept for six years.

You have to remember that it's likely that you will be investigated by HMRC's officials more than once during the average life of a business. When they come to see you, they will be wanting to check that your accounts are in order and that your VAT Returns have been properly prepared. You should arrange your affairs in such a way that anyone can find his way from your original transactions through to the submissions to HMRC without too much difficulty. The technical term for this is an audit trail and we would strongly suggest that you ask a professional accountant for help in making sure that your records are complete and well filed.

VAT Invoices

There are three kinds of VAT invoice:

1. full invoices;

2. modified invoices (for retail supplies over £250.00); and

3. simplified invoices (for supplies under £250.00).

Here is what you have to include in each invoice:

	Full invoice	Simplified invoice	Modified invoice
Unique invoice number that follows on from the last invoice	Yes	Yes	Yes
Your business name and address	Yes	Yes	Yes
Your VAT number	Yes	Yes	Yes
Date	Yes	No	Yes
The tax point (or 'time of supply') if this is different from the invoice date	Yes	Yes	Yes
Customer's name or trading name, and address	Yes	No	Yes
Description of the goods or services	Yes	Yes	Yes
Total amount excluding VAT	Yes	No	Yes
Total amount of VAT	Yes	No	Yes
Price per item, excluding VAT	Yes	No	Yes
Quantity of each type of item	Yes	No	Yes
Rate of any discount per item	Yes	No	Yes
Rate of VAT charged per item - if an item is exempt or zero-rated make clear no VAT on these items	Yes	Yes*	Yes
Total amount including VAT	No	Yes*	Yes

*If items are charged at different VAT rates, then show this for each.

The VAT Return

For most VAT-registered traders, HMRC will be receiving the information via specialist accounting software. However, for those not required to use MTD, HMRC needs just four figures for the VAT Return:

1. **Output VAT (box 1).** This is the total of the VAT you have charged on your sales invoices during the period. If you complete the VAT Return under the cash accounting rules (if your turnover is less than £1,350,000), then your output tax is calculated on the cash received during the period and not on the invoices issued. The figure must include any VAT fuel scale charge for private motoring (see below).

2. **Input VAT (box 4).** This is the VAT that you yourself have been charged on your purchases, etc. during the period. If you are registered for VAT,

then nearly all the VAT you have been charged can be included in this box. If you complete the VAT Return under the cash accounting rules, then your input tax is calculated on the cash paid during the period and not on the invoices received. You may not reclaim VAT on business entertaining, goods or services used privately or on the purchase of motor cars. If you lease a car which has any element of private use, you can only reclaim half the input VAT. If you reclaim VAT on fuel, you must add the fuel scale charge for your vehicle to the output VAT in box 1 (see above). In addition, if you make some taxable and some exempt supplies, you may only be able to claim part of your input VAT.

3. **Total outputs (box 6).** This is the sum of the invoices you have issued to your customers (the sales of standard and zero-rated goods and services) during the period. (You should not include any exempt sales, or any capital introduced.) This sum should exclude the VAT element. However, if you are cash accounting, you total the sum received from **your customers during the period but exclude the VAT element.**

4. **Total inputs (box 7).** This is the sum of the invoices you have received from your suppliers during the period. This sum should exclude the VAT element. However, if you are cash accounting, you total the payments you have made for standard and zero-related purchases during the period, less the VAT element. You should not include any exempt purchases, nor any drawings.

You will notice that there are five other boxes on the VAT Return:

- Boxes 2, 8 and 9 affect few small traders; if they affect you, you should seek professional advice.

- The only other boxes that affect everyone are boxes 3 (the total of boxes 1 and 2) and 5 (the sum of box 3 less box 4 if there is net VAT to be paid to HMRC and the sum of box 4 less box 3 if there is net VAT to be reclaimed by you).

You must file the completed VAT Return electronically and make your VAT payment electronically by the seventh day of the month after the month following the end of your VAT period.

HMRC treat all cheques sent by post as having been received on the date when cleared funds reach the department's bank account.

Fuel scale charge

If you reclaim VAT on all your motor fuel including that used privately, you are deemed to be making a supply to yourself of the private fuel. This supply must have output tax on it, just like any other standard rated supply. HMRC has prescribed values for this supply, depending on the size of your car engine and the type of fuel used. The rates are shown in Appendix 11. It follows that, if the scale charge exceeds the value of the input tax you actually suffer on fuel purchases, you are better off not claiming input tax at all on your fuel.

Annual accounting for VAT

If your turnover is less than £1,350,000, you may apply to HMRC not to fill in quarterly VAT Returns but, instead, to:

- make nine monthly or three quarterly payments by direct debit;
- fill in a single, annual VAT Return; and
- settle up any over- or underpayment with it at the end of the year.

If you do this, you have two months in which to file your VAT Return and pay any VAT due rather than one. Once your turnover reaches £1,600,000, you are no longer eligible to be part of the scheme.

Cash accounting for VAT

If your turnover is less than £1,350,000, you may pay VAT only when your customers have paid you and not on the basis of the invoices you have raised, whether they have been paid or not. Equally, you may only claim input VAT once your purchase invoices have been paid.

Once your turnover reaches £1,600,000, you are no longer eligible to be part of the scheme.

Optional VAT Flat Rate Scheme for small traders

This scheme is for businesses with an estimated VAT-taxable turnover – excluding VAT – in the next year of £150,000 or less. Once you join the scheme you can stay in it until your total business income is more than £230,000.

Those who join the scheme won't need to keep a record of VAT input tax. You simply charge VAT to your customers as at present and record the VAT inclusive total charged to customers. You don't need to keep any record of the input tax incurred on your purchases. You then look up on the list of flat rate percentages the rate applicable to your category of business, you apply that rate to your VAT-inclusive turnover and pay that amount to HMRC.

If you spend a small amount on goods, you are classed as a 'limited cost business'. This is the case if your goods cost less than either:

- two per cent of your turnover or;
- £1,000 a year (if your costs are more than 2 per cent).

This means you pay a higher rate of 16.5 per cent. If you aren't a limited cost business, you use your business type to work out your flat rate.

Whether it would be worth your while joining the scheme will depend on your circumstances. To work out how you would be affected were you to join, you take your turnover for the last 12 months, add VAT and then apply the relevant percentage. If that is less than the total payments you have made to HMRC in the period, then you may be better off joining the scheme.

You will no longer be able to reclaim input VAT on your expenditure. There is an exception to this for capital expenditure in excess of £2,000, on which input VAT may be reclaimed in the normal way.

If you join the scheme within one year of registering for VAT, you can get a one per cent reduction in your flat rate for the first 12 months. There are planning opportunities available for traders who carry on more than one type of business and each would have a different flat rate percentage. The percentage to be used is that which would apply to the business whose activity accounts for the majority of the trade. Where the majority trade has a lower flat rate percentage than the secondary trade, there may be savings to be made.

To join, download the application form (VAT600 FRS – Application to join the Flat Rate Scheme) from the www.gov.uk website.

Table of flat rate percentages by trade sector

Category of business	Appropriate percentage
Accountancy or book-keeping	14.5
Advertising	11
Agricultural services	11
Any other activity not listed elsewhere	12
Architect, civil and structural engineer or surveyor	14.5
Boarding or care of animals	12
Business services that are not listed elsewhere	12

Catering services including restaurants and takeaways before 15 July 2020	12.5
Catering services including restaurants and takeaways from 16 July 2020 to 30 September 2021	4.5
Catering services including restaurants and takeaways from 1 October 2021 to 31 March 2022	8.5
Computer and IT consultancy or data processing	14.5
Computer repair services	10.5
Dealing in waste or scrap	10.5
Entertainment or journalism	12.5
Estate agency or property management services	12
Farming or agriculture that is not listed elsewhere	6.5
Film, radio, television or video production	13
Financial services	13.5
Forestry or fishing	10.5
General building or construction services*	9.5
Hairdressing or other beauty treatment services	13
Hiring or renting goods	9.5
Hotel or accommodation	10.5
Investigation or security	12
Labour-only building or construction services*	14.5
Laundry or dry-cleaning services	12
Lawyer or legal services	14.5
Library, archive, museum or other cultural activity	9.5
Management consultancy	14
Manufacturing fabricated metal products	10.5
Manufacturing food	9
Manufacturing that is not listed elsewhere	9.5
Manufacturing yarn, textiles or clothing	9
Membership organisation	8
Mining or quarrying	10
Packaging	9
Photography	11

Post offices	5
Printing	8.5
Publishing	11
Pubs	6.5
Real estate activity not listed elsewhere	14
Repairing personal or household goods	10
Repairing vehicles	8.5
Retailing food, confectionery, tobacco, newspapers or children's clothing	4
Retailing pharmaceuticals, medical goods, cosmetics or toiletries	8
Retailing that is not listed elsewhere	7.5
Retailing vehicles or fuel	6.5
Secretarial services	13
Social work	11
Sport or recreation	8.5
Transport or storage, including couriers, freight, removals and taxis	10
Travel agency	10.5
Veterinary medicine	11
Wholesaling agricultural products	8
Wholesaling food	7.5
Wholesaling that is not listed elsewhere	8.5

VAT reverse charge

The reverse charge is how you must account for VAT on services that you buy from businesses that are based outside the UK. If you are not registered, the reverse charge will not apply to you. The reverse charge is the amount of VAT you would have paid on that service if you had bought it in the UK. You charge yourself the VAT and you then claim it back; so, the two taxes cancel each other out.

The domestic reverse charge applies to the building and construction industry and came into effect on 1 March 2021. This means that the person receiving the service will pay the VAT due to HMRC and not the supplier.

If this affects you, you will need to notify your suppliers if the domestic reverse charge applies. HMRC has produced a guidance note entitled 'Domestic reverse VAT charge for building and construction services' which lists the services that will be affected and those which are excluded. As with reverse charge, the VAT paid to HMRC can be reclaimed in the normal way.

The tax payable when buying a motor car

New cars attract VAT at the standard rate.

You can only claim VAT back on the purchase of a car if:

- you are registered for VAT; and
- the vehicle is to be used exclusively for business purposes. This condition is virtually impossible to prove. The only people who can normally satisfy this condition are taxi drivers and driving instructors, and motor dealers who are buying the car as a stock item; or
- the vehicle is built to carry 12 or more seated persons and is to be used for business purposes.

The tax payable on fuel

Fuel duty is 57.95p per litre. VAT is charged on both the duty and the product price. So, if for example, the pump price is £1.20, then 20p of this is VAT and 57.95p is duty. That makes total tax of 77.95p. Let's say you have just paid £60 at the petrol station for fuel and used your credit card. How much of that amount goes to the government?

The answer is pretty staggering: £39 goes to the government in fuel duty and VAT.

Deregistering for VAT

If your turnover is not going to exceed £83,000 in the coming 12 months, you can apply for deregistration.

Special Covid relief for hospitality and tourism

From 15 July 2020 to 30 September 2021, VAT-registered businesses in the hospitality and tourism sectors may charge a reduced VAT rate of 5%.

From 1 October 2021 to 31 March 2022, this rate is increased to 12.5%.

This reduced rate is available to:

- Any business that supplies food and non-alcoholic beverages on their own premises; for example, a restaurant, café or pub. You will also be able to charge this reduced rate on your supplies of hot take-away food and hot take-away non-alcoholic beverages.
- Any business that supplies sleeping accommodation in a hotel or similar establishment.
- Certain supplies of holiday accommodation.
- Charge fees for caravan pitches and associated facilities.
- Charge fees for tent pitches or camping facilities.
- Admission to certain attractions, so long as the admission fee is not exempt.

CHAPTER 16

Stamp Duty, Stamp Duty Reserve Tax and Stamp Duty Land Tax

Stamp Duty

Stamp Duty is a tax on documents which applies to stock transfer forms transferring shares. Buying UK land incurs a different tax called Stamp Duty Land Tax.

Transfers of unlisted shares and securities sold on 'recognised growth markets' are not subject to Stamp Duty. Similarly, Stamp Duty is not payable on purchases of shares in exchange traded funds.

For a document to be subject to Stamp Duty it must be signed in the UK, regardless of where in the world the assets are based. A document which is signed outside the UK can be subject to Stamp Duty if it relates to property in the UK or anything to be done in the UK.

Documents have to be sent to the Stamp Office within 30 days of being signed to get them stamped and for Stamp Duty to be paid. Missing this 30 day deadline can incur penalty charges and interest.

There is no direct obligation on a buyer of shares to pay Stamp Duty. However, unstamped or insufficiently stamped documents are not admissible evidence for any purpose other than during criminal court proceedings. Also, a company secretary cannot register a share transfer unless the document has been properly stamped.

Stamp Duty Rates

If you buy shares for more than £1,000 using a stock transfer form you have to pay Stamp Duty. You need to send the form to HM Revenue & Customs for stamping along with the payment.

Stamp Duty is calculated at 0.5 per cent of the value of the shares, with figures rounded up to the nearest £5, and is payable when shares are transferred. It is not payable when new shares are issued. HMRC provides a calculator to work out how much stamp duty is payable.

Stamp Duty is not payable when shares are transferred for less than £1000 (including any connected transfers). This has to be certified by signing the back of the stock transfer form.

Stamp duty does not have to be paid on gifts of shares.

Payment of Stamp Duty

Stamp Duty is payable by the purchaser and must be paid within 30 days of transfer documents being signed. Failure to meet this deadline can result in penalties, interest being charged and fines.

Stamping is carried out in Birmingham. Documents should be sent to:

Birmingham Stamp Office
9th Floor
City Centre House
30 Union Street
Birmingham, B2 4AR

Stamp Duty Reserve Tax (SDRT)

Stamp Duty is a tax on documents whereas SDRT is a tax on agreements to transfer chargeable securities. Chargeable securities include stocks, shares and certain loan capital but shares on recognised growth markets are exempt.

SDRT can apply to the same transactions as Stamp Duty meaning that both an agreement to transfer shares and the signed document to make the transfer can be subject to tax. However, when the transfer document is stamped within six years of the agreement, the SDRT liability is cancelled to avoid a double charge.

SDRT does not apply to the issue of new shares. Purchasers must pay SDRT at 0.5 per cent on the purchase price of the shares.

Stamp Duty Land Tax (SDLT)

SDLT is generally payable on the purchase or transfer of property or land in England and Northern Ireland, where the amount paid is above a certain threshold. Most English and Northern Irish land and property transactions must be notified to HMRC on a SDLT Return within a certain time limit even if no tax is due.

Various rules apply for working out how much, if any, SDLT is payable. The calculation—based on a value called the 'chargeable consideration'— can vary depending on whether the land is residential or non-residential, freehold or leasehold, or on other factors such as whether several transactions are linked.

There are also some types of transaction that are exempt from SDLT, or where reliefs can reduce the amount payable.

SDLT is charged as a percentage of the amount given for property or land when it is bought or transferred, unless there is a relief or exemption.

Higher percentage SDLT rates apply to higher-value transactions.

SDLT Rates

The rates of SDLT on the purchase of residential property are:

Date of Transaction	Residential Band	Charge
1 April 2021 to 30 June 2021	£0 to £500,000	0%
	£500,001 to £925,000	5%
	£925,001 to £1,500,000	10%
	Over £1,500,000	12%
1 July 2021 to 30 September 2021	£0 to £250,000	0%
	£250,001 to £925,000	5%
	£925,001 to £1,500,000	10%
	Over £1,500,000	12%
From 1 October 2021	£0 to £125,000	0%
	£125,001 to £250,000	2%
	£250,001 to £925,000	5%
	£925,001 to £1,500,000	10%
	Over £1,500,000	12%

The rates of SDLT only apply to the amount of the purchase price that falls within the duty band, making it more like the calculation of Income Tax.

Those buying an additional residential property will pay a higher rate of SDLT on the purchase, being 3 per cent higher than the usual levels. This is targeted at buy-to-let landlords but catches ordinary individuals who are unable to sell their existing property before they buy a new property. If the original property is sold within 3 years from the date of purchase of the new property, the additional 3 per cent SDLT charge will be refunded. The purchase of property for less than £40,000 is not caught by this additional charge.

The rates of SDLT on the purchase of non-residential or mixed-use property are:

Property value	Charge for the 2022/22 tax year
£0 to £150.000	0%
£150,001 to £250,000	2%
Over £250,000	5%

SDLT Reliefs

First Time Buyers' Relief

If you, and anyone else you're buying with, are first time buyers of a residential property you can claim relief on purchases where the purchase price is no more than £500,000.

You'll pay:

0 per cent on the first £300,000 and

5 per cent on the remainder up to £500,000.

If the purchase price is more than £500,000 you cannot claim the relief and you must pay the standard rates on the total purchase price.

Multiple Dwellings Relief

SDLT relief for multiple dwellings is available when more than one dwelling is purchased. The rate of tax charged is determined by dividing the total consideration by the number of dwellings. However, there is a minimum rate of one per cent. Relief should be claimed on a Land Transaction Return.

Tax on the Purchase of Property in Scotland and Wales

Land & Buildings Transaction Tax (LBTT) has replaced SDLT in Scotland; further information is available on the Revenue Scotland website at https://goo.gl/Bdjouc.

Likewise, Land Transaction Tax (LTT) has replaced SDLT in Wales; further information on this is available on the Welsh Government website at https://goo.gl/4ka8oH.

SDLT Rates for Corporate Bodies

If residential property is bought for more than £500,000 by a 'non-natural person' (i.e. a company, partnership including a company, or collective investment scheme) then SDLT is payable at 15 per cent. (See also chapter 7 for the Annual Tax on Enveloped Dwellings.)

The 15 per cent rate doesn't apply to property bought by a company that is acting as a trustee of a settlement or bought by a company to be used for:

- a property rental business;
- property developers and trader;
- property made available to the public;
- financial institutions acquiring property in the course of lending;
- property occupied by employees; or
- farmhouses.

CHAPTER 17

Universal Credit, Tax Credits and related matters

Universal Credit

Universal Credit is a means-tested benefit for people of working age who are on a low income. It replaces six existing means-tested benefits:

- Income-based Jobseeker's Allowance
- Income-related Employment and Support Allowance
- Income Support
- Working Tax Credit
- Child Tax Credit
- Housing Benefit.

Universal Credit is being rolled out over a number of years.

Existing tax credit claimants are not affected by the rollout unless they:

- Choose to claim Universal Credit;
- Have a change in circumstances that ends their tax credit claim (and they need to make a new claim); or
- They need to claim another benefit that Universal Credit has replaced.

Existing tax credit claimants are being moved to Universal Credit through a process called 'managed migration'. Anyone who moves through the managed migration process will receive 'transitional protection' which means that if their Universal Credit award is less than they received under the old benefits they should receive an extra element to compensate for the loss. The Government currently expects all households claiming legacy benefits and tax credits to have moved across to Universal Credit by September 2024.

The purpose of Universal Credit is to simplify the benefit system and make it easier for people to take jobs, even for brief periods, without running the risk of losing out financially.

Universal Credit has not replaced: Attendance Allowance, Bereavement benefits, Child Benefit, Carer's Allowance, Council Tax Benefit, Maternity Allowance, Statutory Maternity Pay, Statutory Sick Pay, Disability Living Allowance, Contributory Employment Support Allowance, Contributory Jobseekers Allowance, Pension Credit, Industrial Injuries Disablement benefit, Personal Independence Payment and War Pensions.

Universal Credit is paid on a monthly basis (twice a month for some people in Scotland) to a household, regardless of whether the household comprises one individual, a couple or a family. There is a main element plus additional elements which have to be applied for if a household qualifies. These elements are: Child and Disabled Child Element, Childcare Element, Carer Element, Limited Capability for Work Element and Housing Element.

Universal Credit has a cap applied to make it impossible for people to get more by claiming benefits than the average net weekly wage. For a household in Greater London this figure is £442.31 per week (£384.62 outside Greater London) and for single adults in Greater London without children the cap is £296.35 per week (£257.69 outside Greater London). There are more details on www.gov.uk/benefit-cap-amounts. The childcare element of Universal Credit is excluded from the benefit cap.

Some households are exempt from the benefit cap i.e. those households where Disability Living Allowance or Attendance Allowance are claimed.

With a few exceptions, all claimants have to enter into a binding commitment that in exchange for receiving Universal Credit they undertake to look for and take on any work that is available. There is a lot of 'small print' related to what jobs have to be accepted and there are also sanctions for those who do not comply with their commitment in this regard.

Concerns have been expressed by certain groups about Universal Credit but equally, the huge cost to the Treasury of paying benefits has to be reined in; so that only the most needy and deserving are protected, and those who can work are encouraged and supported to do so

Working Tax Credits

Working Tax Credits have been replaced by Universal Credit for most people. You can usually only make a new claim for Working Tax Credit if you or your partner are already claiming Child Tax Credit. Otherwise, you should apply for Universal Credit if you are of working age or Pension Credit if you have reached pension age. Working Tax Credits are tax free. You will receive payments directly from HM Revenue & Customs (HMRC).

There are several different parts of the credit, which are paid depending on marital status, the hours worked, your age and whether or not you are disabled. Because of this, there is no 'one size fits all' illustration. The basic amount is up to £2,005 a year. If you are in doubt, it's always best to submit a protective claim (i.e. you can withdraw it later if you subsequently want to) as tax credits are only backdated for three months. This can be done online at www.gov.uk/browse/benefits/tax-credits or you can contact HMRC's Tax Credits Helpline on 0345 300 3900 and ask for a claim form. Tax Credit calculators are also available on the website (and others) and by working through them you will have a guide to how much you may be able to claim.

The sums available range from £830 to £3,240. There is a Working Tax Credits calculator on www.gov.uk/tax-credits-calculator.

Child Tax Credits

You can only make a claim for Child Tax Credit if you already get Working Tax Credit. Otherwise, you should apply for Universal Credit if you are of working age or Pension Credit if you have reached pension age. Child Tax Credits are tax free but there are various elements to be taken into account. Given the range of variables affecting eligibility, we recommend visiting the HMRC website (www.gov.uk/tax-credits-calculator) and completing their Tax Credits Calculator. It's worth making a protective claim even if your income slightly exceeds the limit, as circumstances can change

The benefit cap

The benefit cap is a limit on the total amount of benefit that most people aged 16 to 65 can get. The amount your household gets from some benefits might go down to make sure you don't get more than the cap limit. The benefit cap affects:

- Bereavement Allowance
- Child Benefit
- Child Tax Credit
- Employment and Support Allowance

- Housing Benefit
- Incapacity Benefit
- Income Support
- Jobseeker's Allowance
- Maternity Allowance
- Severe Disablement Allowance
- Widowed Parent's Allowance
- Universal Credit

If you live outside Greater London, the benefit cap is:

- £384.62 per week (£20,000 a year) if you're in a couple, whether your children live with you or not, or if you're single and your children live with you;
- £257.69 per week (£13,400 a year) if you're single and you don't have children, or your children don't live with you.

If you live in Greater London, the cap is:

- £442.31 per week (£23,000 a year) if you're in a couple, whether your children live with you or not, or if you're single and your children live with you;
- £296.35 per week (£15,410 a year) if you're single and you don't have children, or your children don't live with you.

Pension Credit

Pension Credit gives you extra money to help with your living costs if you're over State Pension age and on a low income. Pension Credit can also help with housing costs such as ground rent or service charges. It is made up of two parts: Guarantee Credit and Savings Credit.

Guarantee Credit tops up your weekly income if it is below £177.10 (single person) or £270.30 (couple).

Savings Credit is an extra payment for people who have saved some money towards their retirement. This can be up to £14.04 (single person) or £15.71 (couple).

Most people who reached state pension age on or after 6 April 2016 are not eligible for Savings Credit.

You can claim on the Pension Credit claim line: 0800 99 1234. There are different rules in Northern Ireland

The following count as income

State pension; occupational pension and private pensions; most Social Security benefits; net earnings from employment or self-employment less an allowance for half of any pension contributions made; and Working Tax Credits.

There is an 'assumed income' of £1 for every £500 (or part thereof) of capital you have over £10,000.

Contact the Pension Credit claim line for more details on 0800 99 1234.

High income Child Benefit charge

Historically, Child Benefit was paid to all families with children regardless of how much income the household had. But now, Child Benefit is progressively clawed back if either partner has income in excess of £50,000 per year. The claw-back recovers 1 per cent of the child benefit paid for every £100 that income exceeds £50,000. Therefore, all of the Child Benefit is effectively lost when income exceeds £60,000.

It may be regarded as unjust that one household with two working partners each earning exactly £50,000 will still be entitled to the full amount of Child Benefit, but a household where only one partner works and earns £60,000 will not be due any.

If your income is between £50,000 and £60,000, you should continue to claim Child Benefit and accept that some of this will effectively have to be paid back to HMRC. However, if you are not already within the Self-Assessment regime (i.e. you do not complete a Tax Return every year) then you should contact HMRC and ensure that they issue a Tax Return to you.

If you earn over £60,000, you should elect to stop receiving Child Benefit. However, even if you stop claiming benefit, if you find out at the end of the tax year that in fact your income is less than £60,000 you will still qualify for some Child Benefit.

To determine whether your income exceeds £50,000 per annum, please refer to the section 'Adjusted net incom?', below.

Adjusted net income

In certain circumstances, your entitlement to certain allowances or benefits is affected by the amount of your income and certain payments that you make. If you are in any of the following categories, you need to calculate your adjusted net income:

- you have income in excess of £100,000, or
- you have income over £50,000 and you or your partner claims Child Benefit.

1. Add together your total gross taxable income from:
   - Earnings (including employment benefits)
   - Profits from self-employment
   - Taxable social security benefits
   - Pensions
   - Savings income (interest, dividends and property rental income)

2. Deduct any trading or property losses which are relievable.

3. Deduct any gross paid pension contributions (usually old Retirement Annuity policies).

4. Deduct grossed-up Gift Aid donations, i.e. the amount you paid plus basic rate tax relief – £1 grosses up to £1.25.

5. Deduct grossed-up pension contributions which have been paid net of basic rate tax relief.

6. Deduct payments of up to £100 paid to trade union or police organisations for superannuation, life insurance or funeral benefits.

The net result of these adjustments is your adjusted net income.

CHAPTER 18

Tax Planning and Tax-Saving Tips

Tax-planning dos

- Consider buying your own house as soon as you can. Any capital gain on your private residence will be tax free. However, by the same token there are no tax allowances for any losses on sale.

- Make sure you have got good pension and life assurance cover and keep the situation constantly under review.

- Make use (if you can afford to) of the £3,000 tax-free annual capital transfer (i.e. give this sum away Inheritance Tax-free each year) and, if you did not use up last year's allowance, you can give away an additional £3,000.

- Always claim your personal and other tax allowances. This should normally be dealt with for you by HM Revenue & Customs (HMRC) but you should keep the matter under annual review.

- Claim all business expenses you are entitled to against any business income – always keep a chit for petty cash expenses. If you don't, how will your accountant know you have incurred that particular expense?

- Pay your spouse properly for any work done in your business. In the 2021/22 tax year, remember, they can earn £12,570 tax free, although payments over £184 per week (£9,568 pa) will result in employer's National Insurance Contributions being due. The employee will also pay National Insurance Contributions if their earnings are over £184 per week.

- Consult with your independent financial adviser in order to make sure you take advantage of the annual £12,300 Capital Gains Tax exempt amount, i.e. if you can make a gain of this size it will be tax free.

- Make a Will. Use Lawpack's Last Will & Testament Kit or take professional legal advice.

- Think carefully about providing funds to pay any Inheritance Tax on death (term assurance isn't very expensive).

- Plan ahead and, wherever possible, let your accountant know of your plans/wishes so that you can be advised on any tax implications.

- Divide your assets and the related income with your spouse so that the best use is made of Income Tax savings and basic rate bands. If one spouse/civil partner is not utilising all of their personal allowance, look at transferring the permitted amount to the other spouse/civil partner. Note that the recipient must only be liable to basic rate tax.

- Let an independent financial adviser give you the equivalent of a financial 'medical examination'.

- Ask your accountant to give you a rough idea of your tax liability in January and July each year. Then divide the sum by 12 and start saving up for it by transferring the monthly figure to a deposit account. This way paying tax is much less painful.

Always check each year to see if your spouse/civil partner is able to transfer the Marriage Allowance to you, and if you are eligible to receive it. See chapter 1.

Tax-planning don'ts

There is a lot of what one might call 'pub chat' about tax – particularly on the subject of avoiding tax – and quite often the apparent expert is not giving the full picture. This is our attempt to give the tax novice some basic tax information so that he can tell whether the information coming across the crowded smoke-free room (or wherever) is accurate.

1. Don't avoid receiving income because it will have to have tax paid on it. If you earn £1 and pay the taxman 20p, you are still left with 80p and that is 80p more than you started out with. Whether you are prepared to do the work for a net benefit of 80p or whatever is another matter. The main argument, often put forward, that you won't be able to afford to pay the tax on any extra income is a false one. If you receive income and pay tax on it, you are left with something. If you don't receive the income in the first place, you will be left with nothing.

2. Don't put tax saving first. Always put sound commercial or family considerations first and then consider the tax implications of what you

want to do. If you own a business which is making money and paying tax, the key fact is that your business is making money. If your business is losing money and paying no tax, then the thing to concentrate on is not how marvellous it is that you are not paying tax but how vital it is to turn the business around and start making money. In the same way, but on a personal level, don't emigrate to a tax haven in order to save tax. Emigrate to a tax haven if you wish but your reason for doing so must not be to save tax but instead because you would rather live there than in the UK. If you don't like the place, why go to live there? Thus, plan to do what you want to do first and then consider the tax implications.

3. Don't enter into tax-saving schemes, on the advice of either an accountant or anyone else, that run a long time. The law can change, your circumstances can change and either could make a nonsense of a long-term plan.

4. Don't automatically trust trusts. Be very careful about putting your money into trusts (see chapter 11).

5. Don't give all your money away in order to save Inheritance Tax. If you do, what will you live on?

6. Don't make your affairs too complicated. Keep your affairs simple and flexible so that you can (a) understand what is going on and (b) make any changes as and when you want.

7. Don't try to cheat the taxman. Be honest in all your dealings. Keep proper records of all your transactions, especially cash receipts, and declare everything properly. If you don't, you will be found out.

Tax-saving tips for employers, employees and company directors

- Shares: companies can offer shares to staff through a share option or share incentive scheme. The rules are complicated, but the chances of acquiring wealth in a tax-efficient way are very real. Talk to an accountant first.

- Company car: this has become less popular as the taxable benefit of having a car has increased so much in recent years that it's often better to give back the car and have extra salary instead. However, if you are prepared to drive a smaller highly fuel-efficient car, it may still be beneficial to have a company car.

- Company fuel: this is now so heavily taxed that it will rarely be beneficial for a company to provide fuel to its employees. You should ensure that there is an agreement in writing which requires you to reimburse your company for any private fuel used. Better still, buy your own fuel and reclaim from the company that which is used for business.

- Cheap loans to employees: no taxable benefit arises in the case of a loan of up to £10,000.

- In general, all benefits are taxable, but meals provided free of charge (or at low cost) in a canteen on the firm's premises are not taxable if they are available to staff generally.

- HMRC's practice is not to tax expenditure of up to £150 per head on the annual Christmas party or a similar function (that's open to all staff).

- Accommodation: a company may purchase a house for an employee to live in rent free. There may be a small amount of tax due on the value of the accommodation, etc., but the charge will be small in proportion to the benefits provided.

- Tax is not payable on financial rewards to staff for suggestions they may make on the running of a business. However, such 'suggestions schemes' must meet certain requirements.

- Incentive awards: employees can be given non-cash awards for meeting certain targets and, in addition, any tax that these might attract can be paid by the employer on the employees' behalf.

- Pension schemes: employers can consider making pension schemes non-contributory. This way they can reduce payments they make to staff by the amount of the pension contributions the staff members have been making (in other words, the member of staff would be no worse off as a result of this), but the company would have less National Insurance contributions to pay on the lower salary figure.

- Company directors will be able to save themselves a little tax in the form of National Insurance Contributions if, instead of receiving their pay in the form of salary, they were to receive the equivalent sum in the form of rent for the company's use of property owned by the director, dividends on shares or interest from the loan made by the director to the company. However, you should seek professional advice.

- Loans to directors: it's illegal under company law for a company to lend any director money and, even if it's done, there are heavy tax penalties attached to this. Do consider the following points:

  1. You can arrange the capital structure of the company so that at least part of your investment is by way of a loan account against which you may be free to draw.

2. It may be possible to keep certain assets (e.g. property used by the business) outside the company.

- Other benefits: provide tax-free benefits to your employees such as childcare, sports or recreation facilities.

For those moving to a new house while changing jobs

If you move home in order to take up new employment, or even a new post within your existing organisation, the following costs can be reimbursed by your employer without any Income Tax charge arising, up to an overall maximum of £8,000:

1. Bridging finance

2. Legal and professional fees and Stamp Duty Land Tax

3. Travel and hotel costs

4. A reasonable subsistence allowance

5. A disturbance allowance (e.g. removal costs and insurance)

Golden handshakes – advance tax planning

- You might ask your employer to pay part of any payment over £30,000 into your pension (within the limits of the scheme). HMRC accepts that no tax charge arises on such payments and this could enhance the tax-free lump sum you receive from the scheme.

- If you are retiring and your total income will be significantly lower after retirement, it may be better to retire shortly after 5 April so that the taxable part of your golden handshake may be charged at a lower tax rate.

For the self-employed

The self-employed have considerably more flexibility in their tax-saving arrangements than employees, and those who are self-employed are probably well aware of the sort of advantages they may legitimately take. However, here are a few that should not be overlooked:

- If you are starting in business and need to draw all your profit to fund your living expenses, it may not be advisable to form a limited company straight away. As a self-employed trader, you have more flexibility and lower administrative costs. You can always incorporate later.

- A pension scheme is a most efficient way of diverting surplus profits into a tax-free lump sum and pension for the future.

A list of the types of expenses generally allowed is included in chapter 6.

For personal taxpayers – particularly higher-rate

For those with high income (i.e. into the 40 and 45 per cent tax bands), and particularly if it's surplus to requirements, funds can be diverted to the following havens for tax advantages either on initial payment or at a later date:

- Life assurance – investing in a 'with profits' endowment policy that will run for at least ten years can produce a good tax-free return.

- National Savings Certificates – these can produce a good tax-free income. It's always a good idea to keep aware of what National Savings and Investments have on offer.

- Perks in quoted shares – many quoted shares now offer perks to their shareholders and these are entirely tax free.

- National Insurance – if you have more than one source of employment earnings and you are in danger of paying more than the maximum, why not defer Class 1 contributions on one of the employments to avoid making an overpayment?

- Pension contributions – See chapter 5.

- The Enterprise Investment Scheme – you can invest up to £1,000,000 in Enterprise Investment Scheme (EIS) shares and you will get Income Tax relief of 30 per cent on that amount. If you hold the shares for three years, you get full Capital Gains Tax relief on sale.

  There is a 'carry back' facility that allows all of the cost of shares acquired in one tax year to be treated as though the shares had been acquired in the preceding tax year.

  You must hold your Enterprise Investment Scheme shares for at least three years or the relief will be withdrawn.

  Any loss you make on the sale of the shares is available against either capital gains or income.

  You must not be connected with the company (i.e. hold over 30 per cent of the shares or be an employee) although you can become a director of the company and still qualify for EIS relief as long as you were not connected with the company before the shares were issued.

  Deferral relief: in addition to the above, if you have made a capital gain this year, and if you reinvest all that gain in the purchase of EIS shares, you can thereby defer all the Capital Gains Tax payable this year on that gain until you sell your EIS shares.

- Seed Enterprise Investment Scheme (SEIS) – you can invest up to £100,000 in the year and get 50 per cent Income Tax relief on the investment. You can backdate the claim to the previous tax year. Providing you have claimed and been granted Income Tax relief on the investment, you can claim 50 per cent reinvestment relief on capital gains. Providing the investment is held for at least three years and the rules of the tax relief adhered to, there is no Capital Gains Tax on the proceeds of sale.

- A Venture Capital Trust (see chapter 8.)

For young and other low earners

Young people starting in employment have little scope for tax saving (usually because they have a low income), but they should not overlook the favourable Capital Gains Tax treatment available for those who purchase their main residence. Very few people have ever regretted purchasing their own residence.

Don't forget, if you are a low earner, whether in employment or self-employment, you may be able to avoid either Class 1 or Class 2 and Class 4 National Insurance Contributions.

Tax-savings tips for children

Surplus after-tax income transferred by parents to their children is usually non-taxable in the hands of the child. However, where children earn income exceeding £100 in any tax year on capital provided by their parents, the whole income will be counted as that of their parents.

The Child Trust Fund (CTF) was a tax-free savings scheme designed for children. The government contributed £250 for children born between 1 September 2002 and 2 January 2011 and a further £250 (£500 for lower-income families) at the age of seven. The child was entitled to the fund at the age of 18 and there was no restriction on how he used the money. Children with a pre-existing CTF can continue to receive up to £1,200 per annum into their fund. CTFs were replaced by Junior ISAs on 1 November 2011. These provide all parents with a clear and simple way to save for their children's future. Children under the age of 18 who do not have a Child Trust Fund (CTF) are eligible for Junior ISAs. Parents can save up to £9,000 a year tax-free into these accounts. Funds in a Junior ISA are locked in until age 18 and roll over into an adult ISA on maturity, to help foster a long-term savings habit among young people.

Capital Gains Tax planning

- For married couples each spouse will be taxed on his or her own gains and will receive a non-transferable annual amount of £12,300.

- Do remember to maximise the benefit of your annual exempt amounts. To this end you could delay disposals until after the next 5 April if you have already used your current exemption or, alternatively, bring forward planned disposals to before 6 April if you have not yet used your exemption, or split the disposals of some asset, such as blocks of shares, to straddle 5 April in order to obtain the benefit of two years' exemptions.

- Consider whether you can wait until after 5 April to make the sales so as to delay the tax payment by a further 12 months.

- Assets of negligible value: if you hold an asset (e.g. shares in a company) which has lost most of its value, you may be able to claim the capital loss now against any capital gains. HMRC publishes a list of shares and securities in companies that were previously quoted on the London Stock Exchange and that have been accepted as being of negligible value. You can use it to find shares which have been declared as being worth negligible value up to 31 March 2021. You'll still have to submit your claim to HMRC if you own shares or securities for a company shown on the list. A list is not published for unquoted companies, companies formerly quoted on the Alternative Investment Market and PLUS Market or non-UK companies.

- Loans and guarantees: you may obtain relief for losses on loans and guarantees made to people who have used the money wholly for the purpose of their business. Relief is not available if the loss or guarantee arises through your own act or omission or where the borrower is your husband or wife.

- No capital gain or loss arises on gifts between husband and wife, but the recipient takes over the other spouse's acquisition date and original value.

- Gifts to charities: because these are exempt from Capital Gains Tax it's often better, if you intend making a charitable donation of an asset which would realise a gain on disposal (e.g. shares), to consider donating the asset rather than the equivalent amount of cash. The charity may subsequently sell the shares and realise the gain free of tax because of its privileged status.

- Holdover Relief for gifts: this is restricted to business assets, heritage property and property on which there is an immediate charge to Inheritance Tax.

- Don't always claim Holdover Relief – it's sometimes cheaper to pay a small amount of Capital Gains Tax than to hold over the tax bill of some considerably greater sum to the future.

- All gifts are exempt from Stamp Duty.

- If you have assets which you expect will increase in value over a period of time, consider giving them to your children now.

- Main residence: no Capital Gains Tax is payable on the disposal of your home. Taking in a lodger doesn't affect your main residence relief but letting the property can. There are additional limited reliefs available for those who let out a property.

Inheritance Tax planning

- Married couples and civil partners should remember the doubling up of the nil-rate band. Each couple has a joint tax-free band of £650,000.

  There is also a residence nil rate band of £175,000 (each) which can be added to the nil rate band (see above) if you own your own home. This allows you and your spouse's estate to be free of IHT if its value does not exceed £1,000,000.

- It's possible to give away £325,000 every seven years without a charge to Inheritance Tax arising. However, there may be Capital Gains Tax on a non-cash gift, so take professional advice.

- There is tapering relief on the Inheritance Tax attributable to gifts so that, as the years up to seven slip by, the tax bill can reduce significantly.

- It's important to remember, in planning to reduce the Inheritance Tax bill upon your death, not to give away too much unless you can genuinely afford to do so. If you wish to make a gift of your family home but also wish to continue living in it, you must either pay full market rent for the privilege or consult a specialist Inheritance Tax adviser, who may be able to provide a sophisticated planning scheme to circumvent the 'reservation of benefit' rules. With no Capital Gains Tax arising on death, it's sometimes better to let properties pass on death rather than before. However, this matter must be carefully weighed up before a decision is made.

- Lifetime gifts: gifts between husband and wife are exempt from Inheritance Tax.

- Remember, you can give away the annual Inheritance Tax-exempt sum of £3,000, which may be doubled up if the exemption was not used in the previous year.

- Gifts of up to £250 per year to an individual are tax free.

- Gifts out of surplus income are tax free; take professional advice on this.

- Wedding gifts up to certain limits are tax free.

- Term assurance written in trust is a sensible means of protecting a gift that has been made should tax become due as a result of death within seven years.

- Make a Will and build the necessary tax-planning points into it. Discuss this with your solicitor but see an Inheritance Tax specialist first.

- Special reliefs: generally, business assets attract some measure of relief, as does woodland and agricultural property. Agricultural property without a right to vacant possession may attract a lower rate of relief.

- Doubling up the main residence relief: it doesn't make good sense for you to buy a house or flat for your adult children to live in since any gain you make on its subsequent sale will be chargeable to Capital Gains Tax. Instead, consider providing your child with the necessary funds to make the purchase in his own name and you could do this by making an interest-free loan which you reduce each year by the annual £3,000 exemption.

- Incorporation of a growing business: it may be advantageous to give shares in the company to your children and/or grandchildren soon after incorporation when their value is relatively low.

The key difference between tax 'avoidance' and tax 'evasion'

The short answer is that tax evasion is unlawful and tax avoidance is permissible. An example of tax evasion is deciding not to give HMRC details of all your sales (to pocket the cash and not tell anybody about the sales). This is fraudulent and will be heavily punished by the authorities when they discover it. Tax avoidance is taking the necessary legal measures to reduce your tax liabilities to the lowest permissible figure. For example, you may decide to invest in tax-free investments, such as ISAs, rather than in an investment which produces income that is taxable. However, remember that HMRC has certain anti-avoidance provisions to prevent tax being saved as a result of certain activities (e.g. inventing artificial transactions in land). Unfortunately, politicians and others who should know better sometimes confuse the two terms. Of late, there has been much discussion in the media about tax avoidance, and although legal, this too is becoming socially unacceptable. In our view, if tax law were simplified and clarified there would be far fewer loopholes to be exploited.

Communicating with the Tax Office

When we began in practice some 40 years ago, HMRC's staff were portrayed as ogres and inspectors were regarded as 'the enemy'. In fact, in our long years of practice, we have always found we have enjoyed good relations with the Inspectors of Taxes and these bad reputations were both unkind and totally misleading.

While almost all HMRC staff try to be helpful and courteous in their dealings with the public, there is no doubting that dealing with HMRC is becoming much more difficult. It can take a very long time to get through by phone, most if not all of the public enquiry centres have been closed, and their website, while good in parts, can be cumbersome to deal with. There seems to have been a clear policy decision to try to cut costs by reducing the amount of direct dealings HMRC has with the public. Maybe we should all go back to writing letters to HMRC as this is less vexatious to the spirit than their awful automated telephone answering system which never seems to deal with the particular query one has.

Tax investigations

HMRC is very successful at collecting additional tax through its tax investigations and we can all expect an HMRC inquiry into our affairs.

Self-assessment has given tax officers the power to make random tax inquiries. In effect, this means that they have more scope than ever to initiate tax investigations as you may now be investigated even if you have kept proper records.

While no taxpayer will be exempt from a random audit (whether he is an individual or a business), if his accounting and tax records are in good order and if the self-assessed tax liabilities have been calculated accurately and paid on time, he should have little to fear.

When you receive notice that an inquiry has begun, you should respond promptly, courteously and co-operatively. We would normally suggest you seek the services of a qualified accountant.

The benefits of using an accountant

The arrival of self-assessment was, we suspect, originally intended to do away with the accountancy profession. After all, self-assessment implies that the tax laws are so simple that you can 'do it yourself'.

The reality, and we feel that the answers given in this book prove that what we are about to say is correct, is that self-assessment has added to the complications and responsibilities and our view is that anyone having to fill out a Tax Return should seriously consider using the services of an accountant. Not only is life more complicated, but there are now penalties which were not in place before the arrival of self-assessment.

One of the big headlines following the Budget of 2015 was that Tax Returns would become a thing of the past. If you listened to the hype, you might have thought that you would never have to complete a Tax Return again. Unfortunately, the headlines and hype do not really convey the full truth. While the paper Tax Return, or its electronic equivalent, might be being phased out, people will instead have an electronic 'digital tax account'. The plan is for information already held by HMRC to be shown automatically, so that the taxpayer only has to fill in any missing information. While anything that makes a taxpayer's life simpler is to be applauded, responsibility for checking that HMRC's details are correct will still lie with the taxpayer. Fortunately, it will be possible to give your authorised agent access to your digital account.

When using an accountant you should always:

- ensure that the first meeting is free, so that you don't have to part with any money until you know whether you like the person or not;
- ask the adviser to quote for fees upfront and also ask whether it's an all-inclusive service.

For far too long professional accountants and solicitors have churned out bills to their clients based on the hours worked multiplied by the hourly rate. We believe that this approach is totally unfair to the client because the accountant never knows how big the bill is going to be. Instead, we believe that quotations should be made upfront and they should be stuck to, and that the professional should take more risk than has been the case.

Appealing if a tax demand is, or seems, too high

If you think HMRC has made a mistake in your tax calculation, then you should contact HMRC within 30 days of the date of issue of the calculation and ask for an explanation of the figures. If this does not settle matters, you should put your reasons for believing that the calculation is wrong in writing and ask for the matter to be reviewed again at a more senior level. It may also be worth checking your records to ensure that you are actually correct and have not made an error. We are all human and can all make mistakes.

If you are not satisfied with their explanation, or you think that there must be an underlying problem which needs special attention, then you should consult a professional accountant and he will do the necessary.

Support available for businesses and individuals struggling to pay their tax on time

If you're worried about not being able to meet Income Tax, National Insurance, VAT or other payments owed to HMRC or you anticipate that you can't afford to make payments that are becoming due, you can call its Payment Support Service. The staff will review your circumstances and discuss temporary options tailored to your business needs, such as arranging for you to make payments over a longer period. They will not charge additional late payment surcharges on payments included in the arrangement, although interest will continue to be payable on those taxes where it applies. The number to call is 0300 200 3835.

Electronic services offered by HMRC

It is becoming increasingly likely that you will be dealing with HMRC electronically. Indeed, for businesses, any element of choice may already have been taken out of your hands. Some of the more popular online services include:

- Submitting Self-Assessment Tax Returns
- Claiming Child Benefit
- Submitting PAYE information if you are an employer
- Submitting CIS forms if you are a contractor
- Submitting VAT forms
- Submitting Corporation Tax forms
- Submitting a range of HMRC standard forms
- Registering the commencement of your self-employment

How do I register with HMRC to use electronic services?

This is a two-stage process which is started on the HMRC website (https://www.gov.uk/government/organisations/hm-revenue-customs). You will need to have your Unique Taxpayer Reference (UTR) and either your postcode or National Insurance number. On the HMRC website you will register and also sign up for at least one service, for example self-assessment. You will be given your 'User ID' during this process. When you have done this the government Gateway will post to you an Activation Code, which should be received within seven days. When you have both your User ID and the Activation Code you will be able to activate your account. However, the Activation Code is only valid for 28 days and, if you do not activate your account during this time, you will have to go through the application process again.

Email scams

Unfortunately, there are a tremendous number of 'phishing' emails. These pretend to be from HMRC but are in fact fraudulent. The purpose of these emails is to try to extract from the unwary, personal and financial details which the fraudsters can then use to steal money.

HMRC can only contact you by email if you have provided your email address to them. If you have opted for digital communications rather than paper communications, then as a private individual there are only two types of legitimate communication you will get from HMRC: a verification email to check that your address works immediately after you have signed up to the electronic messaging service, and an email telling you that there is a new message for you.

HMRC will never ask you to provide personal or financial information by email; they will not say things like 'Only 3 days to reply' or 'Urgent action required'.

Always look carefully at the email address a message has come from. Look also for spelling mistakes, poor grammar and a broad greeting such as 'Dear customer'. Even if fraudsters have your email address, they will rarely have your name. If you are in any doubt, report suspicious e-mails to HMRC at phishing@hmrc.gsi.gov.uk.

Where does online banking fit into all this?

Online banking facilities are not connected to the HMRC electronic services. However, if you complete online VAT Returns you will also be required to make payment to HMRC electronically. Companies also have to pay their Corporation Tax online.

If you have online banking facilities, then for speed and security we recommend using this method to make payments to HMRC. Always ensure that you provide the correct reference number with your payment.

CHAPTER 19

Making Tax Digital

Aims

The object of Making Tax Digital is to make it easier for individuals and businesses to get their tax right and keep on top of their affairs, eventually leading to the end of the annual Tax Return. Every individual and business has access to their own personalised digital tax account and these are being regularly expanded and improved. HMRC's ambition is to become one of the most digitally advanced tax administrations in the world, modernising the tax system to make it more effective, more efficient and easier for customers to comply.

VAT-registered businesses that have a turnover above the VAT threshold are now required to use the Making Tax Digital for Business system to file their VAT returns. Smaller businesses have not been required to use the system, but that is about to change, as we say at the end of this section.

According to HMRC, the four foundations of Making Tax Digital are:

1. Better use of information

Taxpayers will not have to give HMRC information that it already has, or that it is able to get from elsewhere – for instance from employers, banks, building societies and other government departments.

Digital tax accounts for all will mean that taxpayers can see the information that HMRC holds and be able to check at any time that their details are complete and correct. HMRC will use this information to tailor the service it provides, according to individuals' circumstances.

2. Tax in real time

Taxpayers will not have to wait until the end of the year or longer to know how much tax they should pay. HMRC will collect and process information affecting tax as close to real time as possible, to help prevent errors and stop tax due, or repayments owed, building up.

3. A single financial account

At the moment most taxpayers are able to see a comprehensive financial picture in their digital account, just like they can with online banking.

4. Interacting digitally with customers

Taxpayers will be able to interact with HMRC digitally and at a time to suit them. They already have access to a digital account which will present them with an increasingly personalised picture of their tax affairs, along with prompts, advice and support through webchat and secure messaging. Digital record-keeping software will be linked directly to HMRC systems, allowing taxpayers to send and receive information directly from their software.

Making Tax Digital for VAT

The vast majority of VAT registered businesses have needed to do this for VAT periods that started on or after 1 April 2019. Businesses with a taxable turnover below the VAT threshold can also sign up for MTD for VAT voluntarily.

If you are unsure how to keep and file digital records, there would appear to be three solutions: Either you keep your accounts by means of an accounting program. This is highly likely to have a facility within it for filing the quarterly digital return. Or you can keep your records using a spreadsheet like MS Excel. If you do this then you will need to buy an extra program (it is known as bridging software) into which you transfer your details. It will be from this program that the return can be submitted digitally. (HMRC have a list of accredited suppliers of such bridging software on www.tax.service.gov.uk/making-tax-digital-software) Or you can pay an accountant to submit the figures for you.

If your taxable turnover has dropped below the VAT registration threshold at any point after 1 April 2021 you are still required to continue to keep digital records and send HMRC your VAT returns using MTD-compatible software. This obligation doesn't apply if you de-register from VAT or if you are exempt from MTD for VAT.

And please be aware that all VAT Returns should be completed and submitted electronically – but there are exemptions. You do not have to file electronically if either of the following applies:

- you're subject to an insolvency procedure; or
- HMRC is satisfied that your business is run by members of a religious society, whose belief prevents them from using computers.

Unfortunately, you must still file electronically even if you:

- don't own or have access to a computer that is connected to the internet;
- lack computer skills;
- disagree in principle with compulsory online filing.

If you feel you may require help, you should contact HMRC or a professional adviser.

Making Tax Digital for individuals

The Personal Tax Account brings together each taxpayer's information in one online place, allowing them to access the service from a digital device of their choice and at a time that suits them. It enables them to register for new services, update their information and see how much tax they need to pay.

At the moment, the information that HMRC receives from a range of sources is held on separate stand-alone systems, which can result in customers being asked to report, via a Self-Assessment Tax Return, information that is already held by HMRC. HMRC is joining up these internal systems and will automatically include information it holds about a taxpayer's circumstances or income in their digital account, meaning the taxpayer will not have to do this themselves.

Under Self-Assessment, over eleven million taxpayers fill in a Tax Return to tell HMRC about their circumstances and income. This is a burden for taxpayers and inefficient for HMRC as well: mistakes can be made or the information can be wrong or submitted too late, meaning the right tax is not collected at the right time and HMRC has to take action. This can lead to penalties and interest charges for the taxpayer which could have been avoided.

More effective use of third-party information, that is, information provided to HMRC by someone other than the taxpayer, will reduce the reporting burden on taxpayers and reduce errors, making it easier to declare the right tax. As the Personal Tax Account develops, taxpayers will use it to tell HMRC when things change. Over time, they will no longer need to complete Tax Returns at the end of the year. HMRC are beginning by using information they already hold and will make better use of this by connecting it with taxpayers and displaying it in their tax account.

Please note that from April 2023 all businesses and landlords with an annual turnover in excess of £10,000 and which are subject to Income Tax will also be obliged to keep digital records and submit financial information quarterly to HMRC.

Making Tax Digital for business

Although Making Tax Digital (MTD for VAT) involves the quarterly electronic submission of a business's financial information to HMRC, these submissions do not replace the obligation to submit annual accounts.

As has just been mentioned, the reasoning behind MTD, we are told, is that it should make it easier for businesses to get their tax right. This is because timely and regular submissions are expected to reduce avoidable errors; reduce the cost of tax administration and reduce the uncertainty and worry that businesses face when HMRC intervenes to put things right. It is also intended that, through MTD, intervention by HMRC will happen much more promptly than hitherto.

VAT reporting has been online since 2010 and over 98 per cent of VAT-registered businesses already file electronically. MTD has built on this by integrating digital record-keeping to provide a single, seamless process with quarterly updates sent direct either from the software the business uses to keep their records or by means of "bridging software" for those who keep their accounting records on spreadsheets and the like.

Thus far, only VAT registered business with a turnover in excess of the VAT threshold have been obliged to submit their financial information under MTD but, from April 2022, all VAT registered business will be required to do so under the MTD regime. And please note that, as has just been mentioned in the previous section, from April 2023 all businesses and landlords with an annual turnover in excess of £10,000 and which are subject to Income Tax will also be obliged to keep digital records and submit financial information quarterly under the MTD regime.

Appendices

Appendix 1: 2020/2021 Tax Rates and Allowances

INCOME TAX

BAND	FROM	TO	RATE
Basic Rate	£0	£37,500	20%
Higher Rate	£37,501	£150,000	40%
Additional Rate	£150,001		45%

PERSONAL ALLOWANCES

Personal*	£12,500
Married Couples**	£9,075

*The Personal Allowance reduces where income is above £100,000 - by £1 for every £2 of income over the £100,000 limit. This reduction applies irrespective of age.

**The full Married Couples Allowance of £9,075 is only available where one spouse was born before 6 April 1935 and for incomes up to £30,200 for 2020/21. It is then reduced by £1 for every £2 of income over £30,200, until the allowance is reduced to the minimum level of £3,510. It reduces your tax bill by 10% of the allowance you are entitled to.

PERSONAL SAVINGS ALLOWANCE

Basic rate taxpayers	£1,000*
Higher rate taxpayers	£500
Additional rate taxpayers	£0

*Those with other income of £17,500 or less may qualify for 0% starting rate on savings up to £5,000.

DIVIDEND TAXATION

Dividend Allowance	£2,000
Liability on dividends in excess of £2,000 within basic tax rate band	7.5%
Liability on dividends in excess of £2,000 within higher tax rate band	32.5%
Liability on dividends in excess of £2,000 within additional tax rate band	38.1%

CAPITAL GAINS TAX

First £12,300 exempt, thereafter 10% for standard rate payers and 20% for higher rate payers (10% if Business Asset Disposal Relief applies.)

CAPITAL GAINS TAX (Residential Property and Carried Interest)

First £12,300 exempt, thereafter 18% for standard rate payers and 28% for higher rate payers.

CORPORATION TAX

Main Rate 19%	

INHERITANCE TAX (on death)

BAND	FROM	TO	RATE
Nil Rate Band	£0	£325,000	0%
Over Nil Rate Band	£325,001		40%

A further nil rate band of £175,000 may be available in relation to current or former residences. Nil rate bands of surviving spouses/civil partners may be increased by unused nil rate bands of deceased spouses/civil partners.

NATIONAL INSURANCE

TYPE	EARNINGS PER WEEK	RATE
Class 1 (Employment)	**Employee (not contracted out)** Up to £183 £183-£962 Over £962	Nil 12% 2%
	Employer (not contracted out) Up to £183 £183-£962 Over £962	Nil 13.8% 13.8%
Class 2 (Self-employment)	£3.05 per week	No contribution due if profits below £6,475
Class 3 (Voluntary)	£15.30 per week	
Class 4 (Self-employment)	9% on profits between £9,500 and £50,000 and 2% on profits over £50,000	

VAT

Standard Rate 20%. Reduced rate for hospitality and tourism 5% from 15/7/20 until 30/9/21.

Threshold with effect from 1 April £85,000. This stays the same until 2024.

Annual accounting threshold £1,350,000. Cash Accounting threshold £1,350.000

STAMP DUTY LAND TAX IN ENGLAND AND NORTHERN IRELAND - RESIDENTIAL PROPERTY

			SPECIAL RATES FOR FIRST-TIME BUYERS		
From/to £0	£125,000	Nil	From/to £0	£300,000	0%
From/to £125,001	£250,000	2%	From/to £300,001	£500,000	5%
From/to £250,001	£925,000	5%	Over £500,000	Standard Rates	
From/to £925,001	£1,500,000	10%			
Over £1,500,000	12%				

See also Appendix 2 for changes made on 8th July 2020 in response to the Covid Pandemic.

COMPANY CAR TAX

Car Benefit	The scale charge is based on CO_2 emissions. The annual charge ranges from 16% for eco-friendly cars to 37% for gas guzzlers. There is no adjustment for the age of car, nor for business mileage. Alternative rates apply to cars registered before 1/1/1998. Diesels attract a 4% surcharge, but not over 37%.
Fuel Benefit	As with Car Benefit, the taxable charge for fuel is based on CO_2 emissions. The charge is based on a sum of £24,500 for all cars, not on the price of the car.
Van Benefit	Any age of vehicle £3,490. Electric Van Scale Charge £2,792.
Van Fuel Benefit	£666

CAR MILEAGE ALLOWANCE, ALL ENGINE SIZES

Up to 10,000 miles pa	45p	Over 10,000 miles pa	25p

Appendix 2: 2021/2022 Tax Rates and Allowances

INCOME TAX

BAND	FROM	TO	RATE
Basic Rate	£0	£37,700	20%
Higher Rate	£37,701	£150,000	40%
Additional Rate	£150,001		45%

PERSONAL ALLOWANCES

Personal*	£12,570
Married Couples**	£9,125

*The Personal Allowance reduces where income is above £100,000 - by £1 for every £2 of income over the £100,000 limit. This reduction applies irrespective of age.

**The Married Couples Allowance of £9,125 is only available where one spouse was born before 6 April 1935 and for incomes up to £30,400 for 2021/22. It is then reduced by £1 for every £2 of income over £30,400, until the allowance is reduced to the minimum level of £3,530. It reduces your tax bill by 10% of the allowance you are entitled to.

PERSONAL SAVINGS ALLOWANCE

Basic rate taxpayers	£1,000*
Higher rate taxpayers	£500
Additional rate taxpayers	£0

*Those with other income of £17,570 or less may qualify for 0% starting rate on savings up to £5,000.

DIVIDEND TAXATION

Dividend Allowance	£2,000
Liability on dividends in excess of £2,000 within basic tax rate band	7.5%
Liability on dividends in excess of £2,000 within higher tax rate band	32.5%
Liability on dividends in excess of £2,000 within additional tax rate band	38.1%

CAPITAL GAINS TAX

First £12,300 exempt, thereafter 10% for standard rate payers and 20% for higher rate payers (10% if Business Asset Disposal Relief applies.)

CAPITAL GAINS TAX (Residential Property and Carried Interest)

First £12,300 exempt, thereafter 18% for standard rate payers and 28% for higher rate payers.

CORPORATION TAX

Main Rate 19%

INHERITANCE TAX (on death)

BAND	FROM	TO	RATE
Nil Rate Band	£0	£325,000	0%
Over Nil Rate Band	£325,001		40%

A further nil rate band of £175,000 may be available in relation to current or former residences. Nil rate bands of surviving spouses/civil partners may be increased by unused nil rate bands of deceased spouses/civil partners.

NATIONAL INSURANCE

TYPE	EARNINGS PER WEEK	RATE
Class 1 (Employment)	**Employee (not contracted out)**	
	Up to £184	Nil
	£184.01-£967	12%
	Over £967	2%
	Employer (not contracted out)	
	Up to £184	Nil
	£184.01-£967	13.8%
	Over £967	13.8%
Class 2 (Self-employment)	£3.05 per week	No contribution due if profits below £6,515
Class 3 (Voluntary)	£15.40 per week	
Class 4 (Self-employment)	9% on profits between £9,568 and £50,270 and 2% on profits over £50,270	

VAT

Standard Rate 20%. Reduced rate for hospitality and tourism 5% until 30/9/21 and 12.5% from 1/10/21 to 31/3/22.

Threshold with effect from 1 April £85,000. This stays the same until 2024.

Annual accounting threshold £1,350,000. Cash Accounting threshold £1,350.000

STAMP DUTY LAND TAX IN ENGLAND AND NORTHERN IRELAND - RESIDENTIAL PROPERTY

Rates from 8 July 2020 to 30 June 2021: Up to £500,000, 0%. Next £425,000 to £925,000, 10%. Next £575,000 to £1.5m, 10%. Over £1.5m, 12%

Rates from 1 July 2021 to 30 September 2021: Up to £250,000, 0%. Next £675,000 to £925,000 5%. Next £575,000 to £1.5m 10%. Over £1.5m 12%

Rates from 1 October 2021 to 31 March 2022: Up to £125,000, 0%. Next £125,000 to £250,000, 2%. Next £675,000 to £925,000, 5%. Next £575,000 to £1.5m, 10%. Over £1.5m, 12%

First home buyers after 1 July 2021: Up to £300,000, 0%. Next £200,000, 5%.

COMPANY CAR TAX

Car Benefit	The scale charge is based on CO_2 emissions. The annual charge ranges from 1% for eco-friendly cars to 37% for gas guzzlers. There is no adjustment for the age of car, nor for business mileage. Alternative rates apply to cars registered before 1/1/1998. Diesels attract a 4% surcharge, but not over 37%.
Fuel Benefit	As with Car Benefit, the taxable charge is based on CO_2 emissions. The charge is based on a sum of £24,600 for all cars, not on the price of the car.
Van Benefit	Any age of vehicle £3,500. Electric Van Scale Charge £3,150.
Van Fuel Benefit	£669

CAR MILEAGE ALLOWANCE, ALL ENGINE SIZES

Up to 10,000 miles pa	45p	Over 10,000 miles pa	25p

Appendix 3: Tax Return Checklist

A list of points to consider when completing your tax return:

For Income Tax – Income from:	Comments
Salary/wages	Form P60 from your employer
Benefits received from your employer	These could be in the form of a car, or medical insurance. The form, if you need one, is P11D
State benefits	See statements given to you by the Department for Work and Pensions
Pensions	The figure for your state pension should have been sent to you by HMRC. Other pension details should be on a P60.
Share options	Your employer will have handed you the documentation
Other earnings	
Self-employment and partnerships	There should be a set of accounts and also details of the tax adjustments and capital allowances if appropriate
Income from savings and deposit accounts	You should have been handed the relevant documents by the bank etc. with whom you have placed the deposit.
Shareholdings and unit trusts	Dividend vouchers or other appropriate record
Annuities	Relevant vouchers
Land and property	We suggest that, if appropriate or needed, you record the details using a layout such as that in Appendix 5.
Overseas	Appropriate documentation
Trusts	You should have been given a form R185 by the trustees
Others; royalties, alimony, bonds, etc.	Appropriate documentation
Deductions	
Loan interest	Appropriate certificate
Venture Capital Trust investments, Enterprise Investment Scheme subscriptions, Seed Enterprise Investment Scheme	Appropriate certificates should have been handed to you
Charitable giving and Gift Aid	You should have been keeping a record of these if you need to claim tax relief
For Capital Gains Tax	
Share sales	Contract notes for purchase and sale of the investments
Land and property	Completion statements etc. on the purchase and sale of the relevant property
Paintings	Auction advice slips etc. on the purchase and sale
Business	Completion statements

Appendix 4: Template for Preparing Accounts

This may be used for self-employed businesses and partnerships

Year/Period from _____ to _____

Sales Income   £ [   ] A

Less   **Cost of sales**
                  Purchase of raw materials and stocks   £ [   ]
                  Construction industry sub-contractors   £ [   ]
                  Other direct costs – despatch, etc.   £ [   ]

Total cost of sales   £ [   ] B

Gross profit or loss (A less B)   £ [   ] C

Other income   £ [   ] D

Expenditure (Overheads)

Employee costs: Salaries, wages, bonuses, employer's NIC,
pension contributions, casual wages, canteen costs,
recruitment agency fees, subcontractors (unless shown
above) and other wages costs   £ [   ]

Premises costs: Rent, ground rent, rates, water, refuse, light
and heat, property insurance, security and use of home
as office   £ [   ]

Repairs: Repair of property, replacements, renewals,
maintenance   £ [   ]

General administrative expenses: Telephone (including
mobile) stationery, photocopying, printing, postage,
courier, computer costs, subscriptions, insurance   £ [   ]

Motoring expenses: Fuel, servicing, licence, motor
insurance, hire and leasing, car parking, RAC, etc. membership £ [   ]

Travel and subsistence: Rail, air, bus fares etc. subsistence
and hotel costs   £ [   ]

Entertaining: Staff entertaining (e.g. Christmas party)
customer gifts up to £50 advertising your business   £ [   ]

Advertising and promotion: Advertisements, mail shots,
free samples, brochures, newsletters, trade shows   £ [   ]

Legal and professional: Accountancy, legal, stock takers,
indemnity insurance, data protection fees, etc.   £ [   ]

Interest paid   £ [   ]

Other finance charges: Bank charges, HP interest, credit
card charges, leasing not already included   £ [   ]

Depreciation and losses on sale of fixed assets
(Please seek professional advice re this.)   £ [   ]

Other costs – Please describe   £ [   ]

Grand total of expenses and overheads   £ [   ] E

Net profit (or loss) (C+D less E)   £ [   ]

NB The profit or loss will almost certainly need to be adjusted for private use, disallowable
expenses and capital allowances.

Appendix 5: Template for Land and Property Income

Year to 5 April _____

Gross income from rents

Rent received: name of property	....	£ ☐
Rent received: name of property	....	£ ☐
Rent received: name of property	....	£ ☐
Total gross income from rents (A)		£ ☐

Less expenditure on let premises (NB Some of these items may not be tax deductible.)

Premises costs	Rent paid	£ ☐
	Rates	£ ☐
	Water rates	£ ☐
	Property insurance	£ ☐
	Security	£ ☐
	Other	£ ☐
	Total premises costs	£ ☐
Repairs:	Repairs and renewals	£ ☐
	Maintenance	£ ☐
	Redecorating	£ ☐
	Repairs to drives, etc.	£ ☐
	Small tools	£ ☐
	Total repairs	£ ☐
Finance charges and loan interest		£ ☐
Legal/professional:	Legal	£ ☐
	Agents fees	£ ☐
	Accountancy	£ ☐
	Debt collection	£ ☐
	Other insurances	£ ☐
	Subscriptions	£ ☐
	Total legal and professional	£ ☐
Services provided:	Wages	£ ☐
	Telephone	£ ☐
	TV	£ ☐
	Garden	£ ☐
	Provisions for guests	£ ☐
	Total services provided	£ ☐
	Advertising	£ ☐
Other:	Please describe	£ ☐
Total expenditure (B)		£ ☐
Net surplus / deficit from land and property (A less B)		£ ☐
(Tax already deducted from rents		£ ☐)

Appendix 6: Gift Aid declaration – single donation

Charity Gift Aid Declaration – single donation

Boost your donation by 25p of Gift Aid for every £1 you donate.

Gift Aid is reclaimed by the charity from the tax you pay for the current tax year. Your address is needed to identify you as a current UK taxpayer

In order to Gift Aid your donation you must tick the box below:

☐ I want to Gift Aid my donation of £ _____ to:

Name of Charity _____

I am a UK taxpayer and understand that if I pay less Income Tax and/or Capital Gains Tax in the current tax year than the amount of Gift Aid on all my donations, it is my responsibility to pay the difference.

My Details

Title _____ First name or initials _____

Surname _____

Full home address _____

_____

_____

Postcode _____ Date _____

Please notify the charity if you:

- Want to cancel this declaration
- Change your name or home address
- No longer pay sufficient tax on your income and/or capital gains tax.

If you pay Income Tax at the higher or additional rate and want to receive the additional tax relief due to you, you must include all your Gift Aid donations on your self-assessment tax return or ask HM Revenue and Customs to adjust your tax code.

Appendix 7: An Elementary Guide to Capital Gains Tax and Inheritance Tax and some of the reliefs available

The effect of a... / On the following assets	Gift CGT	Gift IHT	Sale CGT	Sale IHT	Death CGT	Death IHT
Own Residence	None	Normally none, but the gift must be to an individual or to a disabled trust and the donor must survive for seven years. Taper Relief is available after three years.	None	None	None	Taxable – See Note 3.
Business Assets (excluding Woodland)	Taxable See Note 1		Taxable See Note 1	None	None	There may be 100% or 50% relief. See Note 4.
Woodland (Note: Standing or felled trees are not taxable but the land itself is subject to CGT)	See Note		Not Taxable	None	None	None
Let Property				**Let Property**		
Residential tenancies	Taxable. See Note 2		Taxable. See Note 2	None	None	Taxable. See Note 3
Agricultural land tenancies	Taxable. See Note 1		Taxable. See Note 1	None	None	There should be 100% relief
Other business tenancies	Taxable. See Note 1		Taxable. See Note 1	None	None	There should be 50% relief
Heritage Property	Normally taxable. See Note 5		Normally taxable. See Note 5	None	None	Not taxable
Works of Art	Taxable. See Note 2		Taxable. See Note 2	None	None	Taxable. See Note 3
Loans to a business	There should be no CGT		There should be no CGT	None	None	Taxable. See Note 3
Stock exchange investments	Taxable. See Note 2		Taxable. See Note 2	None	None	Taxable. See Note 3
Lloyd's Investments	Taxable. See Note 1		Taxable. See Note 1	None	None	There may be 100% relief
Trusts (Interest in Possession)	N/A		N/A	N/A	None	Taxable. See Note 3

Appendix 7: An Elementary Guide to Capital Gains Tax and Inheritance Tax and some of the reliefs available (cont.)

Notes to Appendix 7.

1. **Business Asset Rollover Relief.** If you dispose of business assets land use the proceeds to buy new assets, Business Asset Rollover Relief means you will not pay tax until you sell the new assets. Instead, the allowable cost of the new assets is reduced by the gain.

2. Other ways of reducing the charge to Capital Gains Tax

   a. **Business losses.** Trading losses may be set against the capital gains of that year or of the previous year but only if they have first been set against the individual's taxable income for that year.

   Enterprise Investment Scheme (EIS). An annual investment of up to £1 million secures Income Tax relief of 30% and Capital Gains Tax deferral relief. This allows you to defer a capital gain you make in the year you invest in an EIS until you sell the EIS investment.

   b. **Seed Enterprise Investment Scheme (SEIS).** An annual investment of up to £100,000 secures income tax relief of 50% and Capital Gains Tax Reinvestment Relief. This allows you to treat a maximum of 50% of a capital gain as exempt.

3. **Nil rate band**

   Assets passing on death normally attract Inheritance Tax at 40% but the Nil Rate Band (See Appendix 2 for the current figure) is tax free. Transfers to the spouse of the deceased are normally exempt.

4.1 Business Property Relief

You can get 100% Business Relief on a business or interest in a business and on shares in an unlisted company (this includes shares listed on the Alternative Investment Market). You can get 50% Business Relief on shares controlling more than 50% of the voting rights in a listed company, land, buildings or machinery owned by the deceased and used in a business they were a partner in or controlled and land, buildings or machinery used in the business and held in a trust that it has the right to benefit from. You can only get relief if the deceased owned the business or asset for at least two years before they died.

4.2 There may be **Holdover Relief** available. (See Chapter 10)

Appendix 8: A template to help you work out your Inheritance Tax Bill and plan your Will

Assets	Rough Valuation	Totals	Who to go to on death
Property and Chattels			
House	£ _____		
Contents	£ _____		
Other valuables	£ _____		
		£ _____	
Investments etc.			
Stock Exchange investments	£ _____		
Cash	£ _____		
	£ _____		
ISAs	£ _____		
Life assurance policies	£ _____		
Other Investments	£ _____		
Overseas assets	£ _____		
Loans to other people, etc.			
		£ _____	
Trusts		£ _____	
Business assets (these may attract up to 100% relief)			
Farm property	£ _____		
	£ _____		
Goodwill	£ _____		
Lloyd's underwriter's assets	£ _____		
Business assets	£ _____		
Tenanted property	£ _____		
Total	£ _____		
Less Business Asset Relief	£(_____)		
		£ _____	
Total gross estate		£ _____	
Less liabilities			
Mortgage	£ _____		
Loans from other people	£ _____		
Other loans and overdrafts	£ _____		
		£(_____)	
Total net estate		£ _____	

Please see the next page for Inheritance Tax calculation…

Appendix 8: A template to help you work out your Inheritance Tax Bill and plan your Will (cont.)

Total net estate from previous page   £ ⬚

Less:

Gifts on death to wife/husband   £ ⬚

Less IHT-free nil rate band   £ 325,000

Less, if available

Deceased spouse's nil rate band   £ ⬚

Less residence nil rate band   £ ⬚

Less deceased spouse's residence nil rate band   £ ⬚

Taxable estate   £ ⬚

Inheritance Tax due at 40% of the taxable estate   £ ⬚

Appendix 9: Personal Fact Sheet

This sheet is intended to help your survivors find all of your papers after your death

Date this sheet prepared	and who else has copies

Full name	
Place of birth	Date of birth
Unique Tax Reference	
National Insurance No.	
Other useful identifiers	

My Will
Made on
Is kept (if at home describe where)
Name of solicitors
Copies are kept by

My executors		
Name	Phone number	Other contact details

Substantial gifts made before death		
Details	Date	Value

Location of other key documents	
Funeral wishes	
Birth certificate	
Marriage certificate	
Insurance policies	
Pension policies	
Property and mortgage deeds	
Bank statements	
Building society statements	

Appendix 9: Personal Fact Sheet (cont.)

Location of other key documents	
Medical card	
Car documents	
Share certificates	
Other investment details	
Biographical details	
Trust deeds	
Leases	
Partnership deeds	
Inheritance tax calculation	
Annuities	

People to contact in the event of my death	
Name	**Contact details**
Accountant	
Solicitor	
Stockbroker	
Insurance broker	
Bankers	
Pension payers	
Employer	
Doctor	
Trustees	

Business affairs	
Details	
Directorships	
Partnerships	

Life assurance policies	
Insurer	Insured amount

Appendix 9: Personal Fact Sheet (cont.)

Employment History		
From	To	Employed by

Liabilities	
Type	**Details**
Bank loans	
Overdrafts	
Personal loans	
Guarantees I have given	
Credit cards	

Debts that I am owed	
Type	Amount

Clubs and organisations that I belong to

Direct debits and standing orders that will need to be cancelled

Other important details

Appendix 10: Tax Reliefs Available for Investment in Unquoted Companies

	Income Tax relief on amount invested	Capital Gains Tax deferral	Tax-free income	Tax-free gains	Income Tax relief on losses	Losses off-settable against capital gains
Purchasing new shares	No	No	No	No	Yes	Yes
Enterprise Investment Scheme	Yes	Yes	No	Yes	Yes	Yes
Venture Capital Trusts	Yes	No	Yes	Yes	No	Yes
Seed EIS	Yes	No*	Yes	Yes	Yes	Yes

*Instead of deferral relief, you get exemption from Capital Gains Tax on 50% of your investment

Appendix 11: VAT Road Fuel Scale Charges from 1/5/21 to 30/4/22

CO_2 band	VAT Fuel Scale Charge, 3-month period £	VAT on 3-month charge £	VAT exclusive 3-month charge £
120 or less	145	24.17	120.83
125	219	36.50	182.50
130	233	38.83	194.17
135	247	41.17	205.83
140	262	43.67	218.33
145	277	46.17	230.83
150	292	48.67	243.33
155	306	51.00	255.00
160	321	53.50	267.50
165	336	56.00	280.00
170	350	58.33	291.67
175	364	60.67	303.33
180	379	63.17	315.83
185	394	65.67	328.33
190	409	68.17	340.83
195	423	70.50	352.50
200	438	73.00	365.00
205	453	75.50	377.50
210	467	77.73	389.17
215	481	80.17	400.83
220	496	82.67	413.33
225 or more	511	85.17	425.83

Where the CO_2 emission figure is not a multiple of 5, the figure is rounded down to the next multiple of 5 to determine the level of the charge.

For a bi-fuel vehicle which has two CO_2 emissions figures, the lower of the two figures should be used.

For cars which are too old to have a CO_2 emissions figure, you should identify the CO_2 band based on engine size, as follows:

- If its cylinder capacity is 1,400cc or less, use CO_2 band 140.
- If its cylinder capacity is from 1,401cc to 2,000cc, use CO_2 band 175.
- If its cylinder capacity exceeds 2,000cc, use CO_2 band 225 or above.

Before deciding to reclaim the VAT on your fuel, you should look at the amount you will be reclaiming and what the VAT fuel scale charge is, to see whether it is worth making a claim.

Appendix 12: Residence and Tax Issues Explained

If you are	Rent arising		Salary arising		Pension arising		Interest arising	
	in UK	Outside UK	in UK	Outside UK	in UK	Outside UK	in UK	Outside UK
Resident and ordinarily resident	UK Taxable	UK Taxable	UK Taxable	UK Taxable	UK Taxable	UK Taxable	UK Taxable	UK Taxable
Resident but not ordinarily resident	UK Taxable	UK Taxable if received in UK	UK Taxable	UK Taxable if received in UK	UK Taxable	UK Taxable if received in UK	UK Taxable	UK Taxable if received in UK
Not resident	UK Taxable	Not Taxable	UK Taxable	Not Taxable	UK Taxable	Not Taxable	UK Taxable	Not Taxable
UK Domiciled	Depends on Residence	Depends on Residence	Depends on Residence	Depends on Residence	Depends on Residence	Depends on Residence	Depends on Residence	Depends on Residence
Not UK Domiciled	Depends on Residence	Depends on Residence	Depends on Residence	Depends on Residence	Depends on Residence	Depends on Residence	Depends on Residence	Depends on Residence

Please take advice on these issues because this area is a minefield.

The following extra points may be helpful:

- Most people living in the UK will be Resident and Ordinarily Resident and UK Domiciled for tax purposes.
- People born in the UK will be UK Domiciled unless they change it.
- You normally have to leave the UK for one complete year to be non-resident for Income Tax and for five complete years to be non-resident for Capital Gains Tax but please take advice, particularly over this second point.
- Visitors to the UK and who spend more than six months here will probably be treated as Resident but not Ordinarily Resident.

Appendix 12: Residence and Tax Issues Explained (cont.)

If you are	Dividends arising		Self-employment income		Capital Gains		Inheritance Tax on assets	
	in UK	Outside UK	in UK	Outside UK	in UK	Outside UK	in UK	Outside UK
Resident and ordinarily resident	UK Taxable	UK Taxable	UK Taxable	UK Taxable	UK Taxable	UK Taxable	Depends on Domicile	Depends on Domicile
Resident but not ordinarily resident	UK Taxable	UK Taxable if received in UK	UK Taxable	UK Taxable if received in UK	UK Taxable	UK Taxable	Depends on Domicile	Depends on Domicile
Not resident	UK Taxable	Not Taxable	UK Taxable	Not Taxable	Not Taxable	Not Taxable	Depends on Domicile	Depends on Domicile
UK Domiciled	Depends on Residence	Depends on Residence	Depends on Residence	Depends on Residence	Depends on Residence	Depends on Residence	UK Taxable	UK Taxable
Not UK Domiciled	Depends on Residence	Depends on Residence	Depends on Residence	Depends on Residence	Depends on Residence	Depends on Residence	UK Taxable	Not Taxable

Appendix 13: Glossary

Additional rate tax	Income Tax at 45 per cent.
Agricultural Property Relief	This only relates to Inheritance Tax. Either a 50 per cent or 100 per cent reduction in the value of the agricultural property in the UK, Channel Isles or Isle of Man can be applied when listing the asset values for probate or valuing lifetime gifts.
AIM (Alternative Investment Market)	This is a Stock Exchange market whereby investors can deal in shares in smaller companies, most of which qualify for Inheritance Tax Business Property Relief.
Alimony	Money payable to a former spouse after divorce.
Annuity	An annual payment to an individual, usually resulting from a capital investment. The regular annual sums cease on death. Due to the payment mainly consisting of a return of capital, only a small part of the annuity usually bears tax at the basic rate.
AVC (Additional Voluntary Contributions)	These are additional contributions by an employee to his employer's approved pension scheme or to a separate pension provider of the employee's choosing (free-standing AVC).
Bare trust	A bare trust is one in which the beneficiary has an absolute entitlement to the income and the capital at any time.
Basic rate tax	Income Tax at 20 per cent.
Bed & Breakfasting	Until the Spring Budget in 1998, it was common practice to take advantage of the annual tax-free Capital Gains Tax exemption by selling sufficient numbers of shares on one day (to realise a modest tax-free gain) only to buy them back the following day at more or less the same price. The 1998 Budget made bed & breakfasting ineffective for tax purposes, unless there is at least a 30-day gap between selling and repurchasing.
Beneficial loan	This is a loan by an employer to an employee at less than the official rate of interest.
Benefit in kind	Otherwise known as 'perks' received by a director or an employee which are nearly always taxed as employment income. Any benefits costing under £50 do not need to be reported.
Blind Person's Allowance	An allowance of £2,520 which registered blind people can claim.
Bonds	These are investments provided by insurance companies with apparently favourable tax treatment on both annual payment and final maturity. The annual payments and maturities are called 'chargeable events' by the taxman.

Appendix 13: Glossary (cont.)

Capital Allowances	These allowances are given to businesses for the purchase of capital assets (usually plant, equipment, machinery and motor vehicles), whereby the cost of the assets can be written down against tax over a period of years.
Capital Gains Tax	This is a tax on either the sale or gift of an asset, charging to tax the difference between the original cost and the value (sale proceeds) at disposal. If you make any capital gains as an individual, the first £12,300 gains are exempt from Capital Gains Tax.
Chargeable event	*See* Bond
Class 1A National Insurance Contributions	These are special National Insurance Contributions payable by employers on employees' benefits.
Corporation Tax	This is a tax levied on profits of limited companies.
Covenant	A payment under a deed of covenant in favour of a charity will normally benefit the charity, in that the basic rate tax paid by the individual can usually be reclaimed by the charity, thereby adding to its income, but deeds of covenant have largely been superseded by Gift Aid.
Director	A director is someone appointed by the shareholders to run a limited company. Sometimes people who are not called directors, nor formally appointed as such, by virtue of the activities they undertake in running the business, take on the same responsibilities and liabilities that a formal director attracts. Directors have certain extra responsibilities under tax law, particularly having to report on the taxable benefits they receive.
Discretionary trust	This is a type of trust whereby the trustees are given discretion as to the way in which they distribute income and capital to the various potential beneficiaries. In the case of other (non-discretionary) trusts the trustees are bound to pay the income over to the named beneficiaries.
Dividend	A dividend is a sum paid out of profits to shareholders of a company based on the number of shares they hold.
Domicile	The country or state which is your natural home. Professional advice should be sought over this, but someone who has a foreign domicile doesn't regard the UK as his real home. This can arise if the individual, or their father, was born outside the UK.
Earned income	This is the income of an individual which is derived from his employment. It also includes most pensions.
Emolument	This is a formal name given to salary, remuneration, bonuses and other income deriving from an employment of a director or employee.
Endowment	This usually is a form of life insurance involving payment by the insurer of a sum on a specified date, or on death.

Appendix 13: Glossary (cont.)

Endowment Mortgage	This is a mortgage linked to an endowment insurance policy with the mortgage being repaid from the sum insured. These have been largely superseded by repayment mortgages in recent years.
Enterprise Investment Scheme	This is a scheme under which individuals receive favourable Income Tax and Capital Gains Tax treatment when investing in qualifying unquoted trading companies.
Filing date	31 January, being the date following the end of the tax year by which your Self-Assessment Tax Return must have been submitted electronically to HM Revenue & Customs if you are to avoid an automatic £100 penalty. The filing date is 31 October if you send in a paper return.
Free-standing AVC	*See* AVC
Fringe benefit	*See* Benefit in kind
Gift Aid	Gift Aid covers individual single donations to charities from which, so long as enough basic rate tax has been paid by the donor, the charity is entitled to reclaim the tax. A form has to be filled in and handed to the charity. *See* Appendix 6.
Golden handshake	Term given to a lump sum payment made by an employer to an employee on the cessation of his employment. This can usually attract favourable tax treatment.
Gross income	Income from which no tax is deducted at source, even though tax may still have to be paid.
Higher-rate tax	Income Tax at 40 per cent.
Holdover relief	This is tax relief given to a donor, or other transferor of business assets, whereby the gain is not charged to tax but postponed. It is deducted from the cost of the asset in the hands of the recipient.
Income Tax	This was the tax introduced in 1799 to pay for the Napoleonic Wars and is still with us today.
Indexation	Available only to companies and only up to 1 January 2018. This allowance provides for that element of a capital gain which is attributable to inflation.
Inheritance Tax	This is the tax payable on assets transferred on death and by way of lifetime gift, although estates (including transfers in the previous seven years) don't pay tax on the first £325,000.
Inheritance Tax Exemption	It's possible to give away £3,000 each year (the annual exemption) with no Inheritance Tax implications. If you did not use the previous year's exemption, it's also possible to go back one year and include that as well, thereby doubling up the exemption to £6,000.
ISA (Individual Savings Account)	A tax-free savings account for individuals.
Lodger	*See* Rent-a-room relief.

Appendix 13: Glossary (cont.)

Maintenance	A term for the payments made by one spouse to another after divorce.
Mortgage	A debt secured by a document (called a 'mortgage deed') which gives security to the lender for the debt. The mortgage deed must be returned at the time of settlement of the debt.
National Insurance	This is a levy applied to employment income and self-employment income, some of the contributions going towards the state pension on retirement and other contributory benefits.
Overlap relief	Where a self-employed person suffers tax more than once on a particular year's profits, a figure of overlap relief should be calculated so that, in due course, usually on the cessation of the business, this overpayment of tax may be taken into account.
PAYE (Pay As You Earn)	The compulsory system for employers to use whereby tax is deducted more or less evenly over the year resulting in the correct amount of tax being paid by the end of the tax year on an individual's earnings.
Potentially Exempt Transfer	A gift made by an individual that, so long as the donor lives for a further seven years, won't attract Inheritance Tax.
Private Residence Relief	This is the relief that exempts any gain on the sale of the home of an owner-occupier from Capital Gains Tax.
Rent-a-room relief	Special relief for individuals who let rooms to lodgers in their homes. Up to £7,500 per annum can be received in rent without any tax liability.
Rollover relief	This is a Capital Gains Tax relief that is available to an individual, partnership or company which disposes of one business asset and uses the proceeds to acquire a replacement business asset during a specified qualifying period.
Self-employed	Someone who is working in business on his own, preparing accounts and paying his own tax and National Insurance contributions. Note: It can be unclear if someone should be classified as employed or self-employed and, in these cases, professional advice should be sought.
Settlement	*See* Trust
Share option	This is an option granted to directors or employees whereby they may buy shares in the company for which they work.
Stamp Duty	This is the duty payable on transfers of shares.
Stamp Duty Land Tax	This is the duty payable on transfers of property.
Tax avoidance	Legally arranging your affairs in such a way as to reduce your tax liability.
Tax evasion	Illegally avoiding a tax liability – evade tax at your peril!

Appendix 13: Glossary (cont.)

Term assurance	This is a cheap form of life assurance whereby, on the death of an individual within a certain specified time, a capital sum will be paid. This can be useful for providing for possible Inheritance Tax liabilities.
Trust (Otherwise known as 'Settlement')	Property is held in trust where the owner has passed it to trustees who hold it and manage it under the terms of the legal deed (called the 'trust deed') for the benefit of the beneficiaries. The trustees are the legal owners while the beneficiaries are the beneficial owners.
Unearned Income	Income from investments and property as opposed to income from employment (earned income).
Unincorporated	Partnerships and sole traders are unincorporated businesses and are not separate legal entities. Limited liability partnerships and limited companies are incorporated businesses and are separate legal entities.
Unit trust	An investment fund investing the combined contributions from individual investors and paying them dividends in proportion to their holding.
Venture Capital Trust	This is a type of investment trust for investing in unquoted trading companies with significant tax advantages for the investor.
Wasting asset	This is an asset that has an anticipated useful life of less than 50 years.
Wayleave	The land and property income deriving from sundry items such as telegraph and electricity poles.
Will	A legal document that shows how a deceased person wished his estate to be distributed, and who was to administer that estate.

Index

Notes

Notes

Notes